THE MILLENNIAL
SUCCESS
CODE

INSPIRE, ENLIGHTEN, TRANSFORM

NOLAN PILLAY

International Best-Selling Author

Ignite Publishing is proud and excited to bring you this book by International best-selling author Nolan Pillay, *The Millennial Success Code.*

As the leader in Empowerment publishing, Ignite's mission is to produce inspiring, motivational, and empowering books that will Ignite the reader's life. They are of the highest caliber to offer engaging, profound, and life-changing information that will impact the reader. Our mandate is to build a conscious, positive, and supportive community through our books, speaking events, writing workshops, Ignite experiences, podcasts, TV shows, and marketplace. We welcome new book ideas and new authors onto our platform. Should you desire to be published, please apply at www.igniteyou.life/apply or reach out to us at info@igniteyou.life.

Published and printed by Ignite YOU Inc.
Canada, T4N1S1 1-877-677-6115

Cover design by ....
Book design by JB Owen and Kristine Magno
Edited by JB Owen, Mimi Safiyah, Steph Elliott and Carissa Simpson.
Designed in Canada, Printed in China
ISBN: 979-8-9910888-4-8
First edition:© April 2025

Ordering Information: Quantity sales. Special discounts are available on quantity purchases by corporations, associations, and others. For details, contact the publisher at the above address. Programs, products, or services provided by the author are found by contacting them directly. Resources named in the book are found in the resources pages at the back of the book.

Author Details:
Email: nolan@straighttalkwithnolan.com
Websites:
https://nolanpillay360.com/
https://straighttalkwithnolan.com/

Social Media:
Facebook: nolan.pillay.37
Instagram: iamnolanpillay
LinkedIn: nolanpillay

THE MILLENNIAL SUCCESS CODE

INSPIRE, ENLIGHTEN, TRANSFORM

NOLAN PILLAY
International Best-Selling Author

DEDICATION

To my courageous parents, your resilience through life's challenges and steadfast values have shaped me into the person I am today. Though my father is no longer with us physically, his strength, love, and guidance remain deeply rooted in my heart. I am eternally grateful for all that you both have done and continue to do.

To my beloved wife, Seema, and my wonderful children, Alicia and Tre, thank you for your boundless love, unwavering support and the endless encouragement you give me every day. You are my greatest blessing, and your presence in my life fills my heart with joy and purpose. Seema, your kindness, resilience, and belief in me inspire me to reach higher, while Alicia and Tre, your laughter and curiosity remind me of life's beauty and keep me grounded in what truly matters. Every moment shared with you brings meaning to my journey, and I am eternally grateful for the love and light you bring into my world.

To my family and friends, your encouragement has been invaluable, and I thank you from the bottom of my heart for walking this journey with me.

Finally, to our Angels in heaven, thank you for your constant guidance and protection. Though you are no longer here, your presence is felt in every step I take.

Your light continues to lead the way.

ENDORSEMENTS

Nolan Pillay is the quintessential warrior man, who breathes life into people through his words. Whether he is writing, or speaking, his authenticity, courage, daring vulnerability, and inspiration have a profound impact on whoever is lucky enough to land on his words. *The Millennial Success Code - Inspire, Enlighten, Transform* will do just that, inspire, enlighten, and transform you in direct alignment with your dreams.

— TIVANIA MOODLEY
Multi-award-winning author of Girl on Fire

Nolan Pillay is not only a wonderful writer but a beautiful human. He came to this earth to make a difference and he lives that every day. I was with him in Las Vegas when he achieved a global award in recognition of his remarkable humanitarian contribution. It was such a proud moment as a fellow South African seeing his stature acknowledged, as Nolan's spirit is one of the deepest humility.

I have watched him soar since writing his first book about his harrowing COVID journey and how his mindset saved him. I have heard Nolan speak on many occasions, and every time, I am struck by the depth and source of his emotions. People are moved to tears when he speaks.

Nolan does not live on the surface; he writes and speaks from the depths of his soul.

Nolan is honestly a living breathing angel disguised in human form. I am so honored that our journeys intersected so I could witness his astounding ascension into the global realm of changemakers whose legacy is etched in selfless contribution.

—ALISON WEIHE
Award-winning Entrepreneur, Speaker,
Author and Identity Intelligence Coach

Nolan is not only an inspiring and extraordinary human being with a beautiful heart, but he is also on a great journey to empower all of those around him. I can say from experience that this is true, and I feel his big positive energy. His work is changing lives around the world and the lives he touches are even more empowered. Getting to know this legend and following his inspiring work and life is an honor. I can only recommend Nolan to anyone who wishes to upgrade their personal and professional lives.

Nolan's deep sense of purpose combined with a global humanitarian vision has contributed greatly to a better society, local development, Human Rights support, Gender equality and Youth Empowerment—a human being with a global heart.

—IVAN GARCIA
English Coaching, Film Producer and Adventurer

Nolan Pillay is my spiritual brother in this world. Nolan and I met through the global Mindvalley community during the pandemic. He shared tirelessly how he was making a difference within his community and bounced back from his near-death battle with COVID. He speaks at events, inspiring people to live their best lives, and with his infectious smile and interpersonal skills, Nolan is a prolific writer, speaker, and overall great human being.

—BARBIE LAYTON
**Quantum healer, Executive coach, Best-Selling Author,
TV Show Host, Speaker, Plus-Size Model,
Featured on USA Today, Forbes, Goss, etc.**

TESTIMONIALS

In this breakneck-speed world consumed by stress for the ever-increasing demand to achieve success, humans, especially the youth, are at a point of meltdown. *The Millennial Success Code* is, for me, the "holy grail" that represents the ultimate success and achievement blueprint and a highly sought-after antidote that will create the foundation and road map to steer humankind towards achieving success with confidence, empathy, and integrity, all with a sense of personal gratification. This all-encompassing success guide with clear, informative, and stimulating content should be introduced as set books in all educational institutions. *The Millennial Success Code* should be in the possession of every individual above the age of 10. I read *The Millennial Success Code* in one night. I found myself saying "yes" to the *Success Principle and Success mindset*, "absolutely" to *Purpose Driven Success and Holistic wellbeing*, and "that's ingenious" to Community and Networking code. Chapter 18 resonated deeply with the core of my being. Nolan is a genius for emphasizing the *"The Honourable Values Code"* *with* "True success is not just about what you achieve, but how you achieve it." I love that Thabiso, a leader and visionary, reminded us to retain our curiosity, imagination, and childlike innocence. Well done, Nolan. I believe this book will transcend and transform the youth and mankind into great future leaders and human beings.

—Shainaaz Dawood Singh -
Founder and Director of Infinite ME (NPC) /
Personal Development and
Human Transformation Company

This is a game-changing read not only for young people but also for anyone who wants to unlock their true potential and reach their goals.

This motivational book is a road map to success, filled with valuable insights and real-life experiences that will inspire young minds.

The Millennial Success Code offers tips and strategies to overcome obstacles and achieve success.

The author highlights that true success encompasses personal achievements and the profound impact one should have on others, leaving a lasting legacy that resonates throughout the world.

Reading this book at a younger age would have been life-changing for me, as it would have put me on a more meaningful path.

Highly recommended.

—Ishara Pillay - Educator, Award-Winning Author, and Inspirational Advocate

This book is a must-read for young people, encouraging them to think beyond the ordinary and view life from new perspectives. The principles shared show how we can tackle challenges by finding creative solutions, just as the author has done. It's especially valuable for students in schools and universities, as it promotes the kind of thinking needed for personal and academic success. I can also relate to many of the insights in The Millennial Success Code within my own business. It has helped me approach challenges differently and find practical solutions, making it a truly impactful and inspiring read.

—Seema – CEO of *Da Wooden Spoon*

In a world filled with uncertainty, *The Millennial Success Code - Inspire, Enlighten, Transform* is a beacon of hope and empowerment. Nolan Pillay has masterfully crafted a guide that speaks directly to those who aspire to rise above societal limitations and embrace a higher version of themselves. This book doesn't just inspire you with the mindset and tools to confidently understand personal and professional challenges. As a CEO under thirty, Nolan's insights are both transformational and practical to me, from building self-worth to mastering resilience. If you are a student, entrepreneur, or executive, this book will help you cultivate a success-driven mindset while staying true to your purpose. A must-read for those ready to take control of their future!

Tremayne – CEO of *Be the BEST version of YOURSELF* Foundation

This is more than a book—it's a movement for those of us seeking deeper fulfillment beyond just career success. As a young woman striving to balance ambition, self-worth, and impact, I found Nolan Pillay's words to be both refreshing and empowering. He addresses real challenges—fear, self-doubt, and societal expectations—while providing practical strategies to rise above them. This book helped me redefine success on my own terms and reminded me that resilience, purpose, and authenticity are my greatest assets. As an experienced professional, I can honestly say that I walked away with a renewed sense of purpose and confidence. If you're looking for a guide to help you grow, lead, and thrive with confidence, this is it!

—Alicia – BI Developer

This book is literally a life hack for anyone wanting to create success and transformation in their lives. It breaks down hard conversations into palatable sections that invite the reader to introspect and unlearn things we've been indoctrinated with while opening the door to new ways of being and thinking. If you're ready to create real, sustainable success and purpose in your life, this is for you. The book gives you step-by-step "codes" to map out your life and gives you the motivation you need if you're feeling stuck. The author's sharing of his emotions and personal stories lends credence to the power of shifting your mindset and what you can achieve when you do.

—Tivania Moodley -
Multi-Award-Winning Author of *Girl on Fire*

The Millennial Success Code by Nolan Pillay is an inspiring and necessary guide for anyone striving to turn challenges into opportunities. As a community builder, activist, and mentor working with entry-level entrepreneurs, I see firsthand how self-doubt, societal pressures, and a lack of direction hold people back from reaching their potential. This book speaks directly to those struggles, offering the mindset shifts and resilience strategies needed to navigate an uncertain world.

Nolan's personal journey, from childhood entrepreneurship to success, mirrors the experiences of many in my community—people with dreams but little guidance on how to turn them into reality. His insights reaffirm what I constantly share with aspiring entrepreneurs: success isn't just about resources but about adaptability, consistency, and belief in oneself.

For anyone seeking to build something meaningful—whether in business or within their community—this book provides a powerful foundation. It's a must-read for those ready to break barriers and create lasting impact. Thank you, Nolan, for this empowering work!"

Arlene Cairncross - Community Builder,
Activist, and Mentor

CONTENTS

A TRIBUTE TO THE MILLENNIAL MAGIC

*M*illennials are described differently by many today. But *what is their true meaning and purpose?*

The Millennial Success Code by Nolan Pillay ultimately defines our true power. I grew up in a different generation, yet his stories and situations resonated with me. I also experienced hardships that I didn't allow to define me. In this book, Nolan shows you the magic you have inside yourself and shares tools that show you how to capture your greatness and channel it. Nolan shares this through the various *Success Codes* in the book, which will help you to own your power.

This book is an everyday rule book through which he navigates his journey to success. His trials, tribulations, and experiences may take you on a familiar road, but they also show you how to rise above anything.

I have always admired Nolan for his passion and perseverance. One of his other books, *My Covid Journey*, was so inspirational. Upon meeting him and following his successful journey and achievements, I can confidently say that Nolan is a man who is always *"Vibrationally High."*

If you ever want to have a rule book of life, *The Millennial Success Code* is it! Millennials, this one is for you! In life, you always want to do what's best for you to achieve your various desired goals, and this book is your guide to ensure that it happens.

I absolutely loved reading this book, and it's a must-read for everyone! You will resonate with it, and if you have forgotten your purpose, Nolan illuminates the path ahead with his *Success Codes*. He reminds you of who you are and who you are supposed to be. This book is a reminder when you go off path in your map of life, saying, *"Here is your atlas – let me show you where you need to go."*

Nolan Pillay is the ultimate inspiration for others through his positive methods of success. He is a symbol of hope and inspires you with the desire to embrace your greatness. I am very proud of him and thankful to be given this opportunity to write this foreword.

Feel Your Power!
Own Your Magic!
Go over the Codes!
Be the Millennial You Are Supposed to Be!

Bhavna Govender
Radio Presenter, CEO Masala JIVE, Artist,

WHO COULD BENEFIT FROM THE
MILLENNIAL SUCCESS CODE?

This book is for those of you who are ready to take their life to the next level. It's for the youth, students, young professionals, employees, C-suite young executives, and anyone going through challenges who are eager to break free from limitations and reach their full potential. If you seek more than just financial success; if you want personal fulfillment, societal impact, and resilience, this book was written for you!

Below is a breakdown of others who could also benefit.

1. **Entrepreneurs and Startups** - Millennials who are building their own businesses can value learning about resilience, adaptability, and personal mastery.
2. **Freelancers and Gig Workers** - Individuals navigating the gig economy and freelancing world might seek guidance on personal growth and overcoming challenges.
3. **Career Changers** - Those looking to pivot into new careers, industries, or roles might resonate with your focus on transformation.

4. **Mental Health Advocates** - People actively working on their mental health or supporting others could benefit from insights into resilience and mastery.

5. **Coaches and Mentors** - Those who guide others in personal and professional development could use these principles to enhance their coaching approach.

6. **Educators and Trainers** - Professionals who teach or train others could apply the book's content in their work with millennials and younger generations.

As the author and someone committed to empowerment, I was inspired me to format the book with reflection pages, and stories. It is my desire to make this a truly immersive experience. I want to create something that would not only guide you with practical steps but also resonate emotionally, giving you space to reflect, connect with your deeper purpose, and feel encouraged to make transformative changes. This book is not just a read; it's a journey to inspire, enlighten, and transform yourself, both personally and professionally.

PREFACE

There was a time in my life when success felt like something meant for other people, those with better opportunities, more resources, or a head start in life. However, I have learned that success is not about where you come from; it is about where you are *willing* to go. I did not have the luxury of privilege or a simple path. I grew up in a one-bedroom home, selling food in the streets to help put a meal on the table. I have felt the sting of failure, the weight of disappointment, and the doubt that creeps in when life knocks you down. But I also discovered something powerful; your circumstances do not define you, your mindset does.

This book is not just about success as the world defines it. It is about a new way of thinking, a new way of being, and a new way of leading your life with purpose, clarity, and impact. *The Millennial Success Code* was born from my journey of struggle, transformation, and relentless self-discovery. It is the blueprint I used to shift from uncertainty to confidence, from struggle to achievement, and from *simply existing* to *truly living.*

Over the years of working with clients, especially those from the millennial generation, I've noticed a significant shift in expectations, demands, needs, and desires within the workplace. What once worked or was considered acceptable no longer holds true. Being good at something used to be enough. Now, people who are skilled and competent are being let go, dismissed, overlooked, or never even given the chance to get their foot in the door. Today, success demands more than it ever has before. It often comes at the cost of personal values, self-care, and emotional stability. It shouldn't have to be that way. This growing imbalance inspired me to write this book to help redefine success in a way that supports both professional growth and personal well-being.

We live in a time where the rules of success are changing. What worked for past generations does not always apply today. Millennials and young professionals face unique challenges. They deal with rapid change, financial instability, burnout, and an overwhelming sense that they should already have it all figured out. If that pressure sounds familiar, you are in the right place.

The Millennial Success Code is about breaking free from limitations, designing your own version of success, and building a life of meaning, *not just achievement*. Inside these pages, I will share the principles that helped me create my success, climb Kilimanjaro twice, become an international best-selling author, *twice*, and most importantly, build a legacy that uplifts others.

This is not just my story. This is about you, your untapped potential, your ability to rise, and your responsibility to lead with purpose. If you are ready to break through self-doubt, transform your mindset, and create lasting success, this is the book for you.

Much Love and Light,

Nolan Pillay

PUBLISHER'S NOTE

By Lady JB Owen

People typically define millennials, also known as Generation Y, as individuals born between 1981 and 1996. At the time of printing this book, millennials are between twenty-eight and forty-three years old. When I was that age, the word *millennial* did not yet exist, but the trials of life, the difficulties one endured, the professional terrain, the outside pressures, and the need to be successful were certainly evident.

At nine years old, I started my first business selling handmade necklaces to people who visited the local pub in my town. I would sit on the steps in the driveway and talk to people as they entered. I mostly targeted couples, asking if the gentleman would like to buy a necklace for his sweetie. Nine times out of ten, they would stop to see what I had. She would pick one, I would put it around her neck, and as she batted her eyelashes, and I delivered a compliment, he would generously buy it for her. His gestures made her happy, he would walk away feeling appreciated, and I would walk away with a few dollars in my pocket.

That simple exchange was my first taste of entrepreneurship. It was innocent, fulfilling, and full of genuine human connection. At that age, I knew nothing of profit margins, market saturation, or economic downturns. I was not weighed down by self-doubt or societal expectations. I simply had an idea, put it into action, and enjoyed the process of seeing it come to life. As I grew older, I learned that success was not just about having a good idea. It required resilience, a strong mindset, and the ability to adapt when things didn't go as planned. The challenges became greater, the stakes higher, and the road to success far less predictable.

This is the reality millennials face today. Unlike any generation before them, they are navigating a new world. They grew up in an era of rapid technological advancements, watched economies rise and fall, and entered adulthood in a time of uncertainty and change. Despite being told they can be anything, they often feel lost amidst a sea of possibilities. With more tools, resources, and opportunities than prior generations, they still struggle with self-doubt, anxiety, and relentless societal pressure.

This is why Nolan Pillay's book is so important.

Nolan is not just another voice in the world of personal development. He is a living example of what it means to take control of your destiny, to push through adversity, and to create a life of impact and purpose. His story is one of resilience, courage, and transformation.

From humble beginnings, facing financial struggles, and battling moments of self-doubt, he emerged as a leader, mentor, and change-maker. Through his own journey, Nolan has developed a blueprint for success, one that is not just about making money or achieving titles, but about true, lasting fulfillment. His *Millennial Success Code* is a roadmap that helps people move beyond fear, self-doubt, and stagnation. It teaches them how to cultivate a mindset of abundance, resilience, and purpose. It is for anyone who has ever questioned their path, felt stuck, or wondered if they are capable of something greater. It is for the dreamers, the doers, the seekers, and the leaders who are ready to step into their full potential. What I admire most about Nolan is his deep commitment to service. He does not just teach success principles; he lives them. Whether it is climbing Mount Kilimanjaro with a team of deaf individuals to prove that anything is possible, mentoring young professionals on their journey to success, or using his own setbacks as lessons to inspire others, Nolan walks the talk. The *Millennial Success Code* is not about quick fixes or temporary motivation. It is about shifting your entire way of thinking, adopting new habits, and committing to lifelong growth. It is about understanding that success is not a destination, rather a continuous journey of learning, evolving, and becoming.

As you read this book, I encourage you to approach it with an open mind and a willing heart. Let Nolan's words challenge you, inspire you, and push you to think differently. Reflect on your own journey. *Where have you held yourself back? Where have you let fear or self-doubt dictate your choices? Where have you played small when you knew you were capable of so much more?*

The answers to those questions will shape your future.

There is a reason you picked up this book. Something inside of you is ready for more. You may not have all the answers yet, but you are taking the first step toward unlocking your true potential. That is the beauty of growth. It does not happen all at once but in small, consistent shifts that eventually lead to a massive transformation. I have had the honor of mentoring and working alongside some of the most brilliant minds, innovative thinkers, and passionate changemakers in the world. And I can say with absolute certainty that the people who create the greatest impact are not always the smartest, the richest, or the most talented. They are the ones who refuse to give up. They are the ones who embrace the unknown, take risks, and believe in themselves even when no one else does.

That is what this book will help you do.

Nolan has given you a gift. He has poured his years of experience, his wisdom, and his passion into these pages to help *you* rise. Whether you are a millennial, an aspiring entrepreneur, or someone who simply wants more from life, the tools in this book will help you move forward with clarity and confidence. Your success is not just about you. It is about the lives you will impact, the people you will inspire, and the legacy you will leave behind. When you commit to being the best version of yourself, you create a ripple effect that extends far beyond what you can see.

As you turn the page and dive into this journey, know that you are not alone. You are part of a generation that is redefining success, breaking barriers, and igniting the future of humanity.

It all starts with you.

Blessings on your journey,

Lady JB Owen

INTRODUCTION

Welcome To Your Success Guide, A Map Specifically
For Millennials.

Welcome to a journey of transformation and self-discovery. In the following pages, you will embark on a profound exploration of your mindset, a terrain shaped by your unique experiences, challenges, interactions, and aspirations during this pivotal time in history.

I can only imagine that you have picked up this book because you have found that in your life, you are facing these very challenges and have not been given the tools you need to navigate them effectively. As you look around, you might see how millennials across the globe are facing potential chaos arising from a lack of employment opportunities, reduced civil liberties, divided gender equality, negative mental attitudes, limiting beliefs, low self-esteem, societal expectations, fear, and lack of direction. Prioritizing job creation and empowering aspiring minds with the right tools, techniques, and a winning *Success Code* is not just a necessity but a crucial step toward harnessing a demographic dividend that could emerge to form a more cohesive world.

Many of you have observed a lack of essential life values, a loss of humanity, forgotten self-worth, and dwindling gratitude within our societies. Instead of nurturing positivity and growth, human conditioning often veers toward negativity and destruction. This is why finding and utilizing a *Success Code* is essential. This book centers on awakening purpose, expanding beliefs, living authentically, transcending barriers, turning failure into success, and clarifying values and goals while inspiring, enlightening, and transforming oneself. It is not like other books that only speak to philosophies and ideas; this book is specifically for individuals like you who want to navigate and overcome the unique challenges you face to become the best version of yourself.

This book addresses the obstacles you encounter and focuses on unraveling the secrets to fortifying self-esteem and nurturing self-worth while building the foundation for a resilient and empowered self. Beyond the confines of traditional career achievements, the success you will learn about here encompasses a multidimensional approach. This journey will blend individual happiness, community impact, and a continuous pursuit of personal growth.

In *The Millennial Success Code - Inspire, Enlighten, Transform,* you will learn how to embrace the essence of your personal evolution. Here, I show you how to utilize the intricate pathways of the human mind, illuminating the route toward the best expression of yourself. By focusing on your inherent gifts, I help you navigate the expansive landscapes of self-discipline, effective communication, and the resilience necessary to confront life's trials. Within each chapter, you will bid farewell to the constraints of limiting beliefs and fears, transcending toward personal mastery and continuous growth. Setting and achieving meaningful goals will become your guiding star. This book is more than a mere guide, it is also a compass in your pursuit of profound change. It delves into the heart of personal development, steering away from the gravitational pull of negativity and embracing the light of positivity and optimism. By addressing the complex web of societal expectations and identity-related challenges, learning the *Millennial Success Code* will help you develop a deeper understanding of your potential that will illuminate the way forward.

Living intentionally becomes a beacon guiding you through uncharted territories of meaningful self-discovery in a world often crowded with pressures and uncertainties. What I have discovered in my decades of working with young people and my extensive research for this book is that millennial success is more than a checklist of accomplishments; it is woven from personal fulfillment, societal contribution, and professional strides. As a millennial, you want more than just to succeed; you seek meaning, impact, and continuous growth. You understand that true success involves a harmonious blend of individual happiness, community impact, and professional achievement.

I trust you are not here because you lack ambition, but because you desire deeper fulfillment. You aspire to make a meaningful difference, to grow continuously, and to live authentically. You are ready to learn new ways to overcome obstacles, expand your horizons, and unleash your full potential.

I invite you to explore the intricate layers of success and discovery, diving deep into the essence of what it means to thrive in every aspect of life. Allow this book to help you unravel the secrets of achieving a balanced life where personal joy meets professional excellence and where societal contributions amplify your sense of purpose. I will help you learn to turn failures into stepping stones and cultivate the resilience needed to rise above adversity. By embracing this journey, you'll uncover tools and strategies that empower you to harness your strengths, nurture your self-worth, and, ultimately, guide you toward realizing your unlimited potential.

This is not just a book; it's a transformative experience designed to help you become the best version of yourself.

ORIGINS OF THE CODE

Where It All Began And Why The Success Codes Are So
Important And Meaningful.

In the heart of a small town, amidst humble beginnings and daunting odds stacked against my family and me, I discovered the resilience of confronting daily challenges head-on. At the tender age of ten, my siblings and I would set out each morning, selling Indian delicacies made by my mother. The intention was to earn enough for our daily meal. As my school years advanced, I took on part-time jobs as a petrol attendant and at a grocery store, striving to contribute to my family's finances.

Growing up in a poverty-stricken environment was difficult. I still remember our one-bedroom home with a kitchen, living room, and outside toilet. The living area had to be divided using a makeshift curtain so we could have a private area for my four siblings and me to sleep in. A thin blanket was our mattress on the cemented floor where we all slept huddled together. Nonetheless, what we had sufficed, and we were grateful to have a roof over our heads.

Doing homework was a challenge, especially at night, as we used a very small candle for light because our parents could not afford to pay the electricity bill. Going to school on a cold, rainy day without shoes or a jacket was also a challenge; I could feel that biting cold piercing through my body. I endured many hardships due to our financial struggles. Yet, when I think back, I realize those experiences were there to mold me and teach me how to develop my fortitude.

Amidst those difficulties, I also struggled in school. I had considered myself an average student throughout my schooling years until I had to write my grade twelve exams, which marked a pivotal but disappointing moment as I failed to pass. This triggered a profound personal struggle that cost me the opportunity to go to college, shattered my confidence and belief in myself, and nearly cost me the chance to become employed.

As I stepped into young adulthood, perseverance and a resilient mindset became my guiding light, helping me overcome those lessons learned through adversity. Financial constraints were a constant challenge that hindered my pursuit of further education, compelling me to take a job as a packer and sweeper in a factory. Although that was not what I dreamed of for my future, I found gratitude in doing the work. Through each demanding circumstance, I discovered an unwavering determination to carve out a brighter future and become the best version of myself, working tirelessly while studying and juggling life's responsibilities. I was on the brink of my life, a young man forging a future at the start of what would become my path. I knew how important this time in my life was, as it would set the tone and trajectory for who I could become. With conviction and determination, I realized I needed a *Success Code* to help me navigate the challenges and opportunities ahead. Forging such a code became my compass, guiding me to harness my strengths, remain resilient in the face of adversity, and stay true to my personal values. Discovering such a code of success and building it empowered me to lead with authenticity, make impactful decisions, and ultimately add value to the world. By adhering to this dedicated code, I could build a foundation for a meaningful and successful life, ensuring that I could leave behind a legacy that would inspire and uplift future generations.

Living with the intention to improve my life marked a turning point for me, a testament to my unwavering dedication toward self-development and learning more about who I was intrinsically. My hunger for personal growth was like a runaway train; I vowed never to surrender, holding onto faith and belief in myself as I navigated through life's complexities. A burning desire and personal conviction empowered me to achieve my aspirations, leading me to start my first company, *StraightTalkWithNolan*. There, I focused on creating personal mastery programs tailored to millennials, guiding them through their own transformative journeys. I devised programs designed to help young people who were budding entrepreneurs or emerging professionals on how to overcome the daily challenges they faced, enabling them to reach their fullest potential and make a significant impact on the world.

My personal voyage of self-discovery revealed untapped potential, breaking free from the limitations imposed by my upbringing. Engaging in various self-growth programs opened my eyes to a world of possibilities, programs like *Millionaire Mind Intensive*™, *Enlightened Warrior Power*™, *Train the Trainer with T. Harv Eker*™, *Thinking into Results*™, *and Paradigm Shift with Bob Proctor*™, *MY Comeback Challenge*™, *Date with Destiny with Tony Robbins*™, *Be Extraordinary*™, *Silva UltraMind System*™, *Super Brain*™, *Speak & Inspire*™, *Life Visioning Mastery*™, *Mastering Authentic Networking*™, *Personal Mastery*™, *The Integral Life* with various teachers at *Mindvalley*™, *Think and Grow Rich*™ with *the Napoleon Hill Foundation,* and *Ignite Your Solo Book*™ program with *Ignite Publishing*™, which was the catalyst for this book. Each of these programs brought about an astounding transformation in my personal and professional life, all sparked by a simple shift in my mindset. The knowledge I gained was priceless, but I had to apply it in my life to see the results.

While observing the challenges I faced during my youth and seeing the work I needed to do as an adult to lay the foundation for success, I thought deeply about how my life would have been different if I had the tools and strategies I needed at a much younger age. Each personal awakening I had struck a chord within me and led me to create a more meaningful life. It became clear that waiting for change to arrive while holding the power to encourage change would be hypocritical. I recognized I could empower young minds, enabling them to transform their lives and contribute to uplifting the world. I knew if I could teach the youth how to chart their destinies based on winning concepts, proven strategies, and a powerful *Success Code,* they could go out into the world better equipped than I was and shape their successful futures.

With a desire to share all that I had learned and help others, I further put my *Success Code* to the test. I set goals for myself that were once a dream and used the code to reach the results. One of those dreams was to become an international best-selling author; today, I am proud to be a two-time international best-selling author. Another dream was to climb Mount Kilimanjaro, and I made it to the summit more than once—the second time I stood at the top was even more impactful and purposeful than the first, as I took five Deaf people on this journey, allowing their dreams to become a reality. That climb allowed us to raise funds and give the gift of hearing to children born deaf, allowing them to live a normal life. I used the *Success Code* to set clear goals, provide direction and motivation, and guide my efforts toward tangible achievements. These goals meant taking consistent action like learning basic sign language and understanding the Deaf community.

I have witnessed the cumulative effect of sustained effort leading to progress and success by doing these steps. Embracing failure has been transformative, allowing me to learn from setbacks, adapt to changes, and ultimately grow stronger. Maintaining a positive mindset has been crucial in navigating challenges, enabling me to persevere and remain resilient amidst adversity. Most importantly, prioritizing continuous learning has empowered me to evolve and stay relevant, equipping me with the skills and knowledge needed to seize new opportunities and thrive in this ever-changing world.

Having a *Success Code* became more than just a way of living and turned into a true lifeline for me. Amid the pandemic, when I was deathly ill and clinging to life in a hospital, I willed every cell in my body to heal so I could walk out of there and not succumb to the sickness. It infused my spirit with courage, my body with vitality, and my mind with clarity, enabling me not only to survive but to thrive amidst adversity. Having my code was not just a roadmap to success; it was a lifeline that anchored me to purpose, propelled me forward, and ultimately transformed my entire being. It is a vital aspect of my life that is deeply ingrained in my daily existence, guiding my every decision and action, providing me with a sense of purpose and direction, and empowering me to navigate life's challenges with resilience and determination. The code is my source of strength, reminding me of my innate potential and fueling my drive to persevere. It influences my professional endeavors, my personal relationships, and overall well-being, shaping me into a more confident and fulfilled individual. In essence, *The Success Code* is not just a part of my life. It is the foundation upon which I built my journey toward growth, fulfillment, and success.

Each of those moments was a testament to the power of my human potential, allowing me to realize that having a *Success Code* is essential and needs to be instilled in everyone. Each one of those situations increased my awareness that sharing my *Success Code* was my destiny.

If you have dreams and aspirations, learning how to use the *Success Code* will benefit you by giving you a head start in your journey through life, and turning your goals into a reality. Using the code will help you move beyond the conventional measures of success; it embraces a holistic path, intertwining personal fulfillment, community contribution, and ongoing evolution. My goal is that this book speaks to those stepping into their years of uncertainty, where success often appears as an elusive concept, especially for millennials navigating a landscape marked by rapid change and unprecedented challenges. I want this book and the codes within it to become a formative guide for those ready to achieve their aspirations. What is within these pages will provide an opportunity to redefine one's success, transcend traditional boundaries, and forge a path that blends personal fulfillment with societal impact and professional achievement.

Using the *Millennial Success Code* I have developed, you can shift from having limiting beliefs, fear, self-doubt, lack of direction, and lack of persistence to a mindset of excellence that is focused on living a purpose-driven life, committed to growth, gratitude, abundance, resilience, continuous self-discovery, and constant learning while finding enlightenment and inner transformation. The code helps individuals navigate the complexities of the modern world with clarity, purpose, and authenticity. Without any doubt, *The Success Code* can shift anyone from a life of stagnation to a life of purpose and abundance.

You are our future, and by implementing what is inside the *Millennial Success Code,* you will become a future leader poised to make a profound impact by authentically leading with purpose and values. Your unique perspective and skills will add value to society, leaving behind a legacy that inspires positive change and shapes the world for generations to come. If you are that person *and I believe you are*, get ready to learn how to believe in yourself and reach the greatest success you have ever known.

By turning this page, you are embarking on the journey toward all the success you desire to achieve.

LEARNING THE CODE:
A GUIDE TO YOUR SUCCESS

Setting The Tone For The Journey And Getting
The Most Out Of Your Success

Let's face it: *millennials learn quickly and want results.* They consume and process information swiftly and like to execute. They don't waste time or spend unneeded energy on long, drawn-out concepts or over-extrapolation. They want to get to the heart of the matter so they can implement it. In writing this book, I knew if I was going to teach this demographic, I needed to share how millennials like to learn; *concisely and to the point.*

As you begin to read through this book, you'll find a carefully structured journey designed to help you unlock your full potential in a way that serves your learning preference. This book is organized into easy, manageable, shorter chapters, focusing on each aspect of a *Success Principle,* a *Success Mindset's* implementation, and a *Success Code.* By breaking down fundamental ideas into digestible pieces, you'll be able to absorb and implement the principles more effectively, making your path to personal and professional growth smoother and more achievable.

The structure of this book is designed to help you stay engaged and make steady progress. Each chapter includes *real-life examples, practical exercises,* and *actionable steps* to help you integrate the principles and mindsets into your daily life. This straightforward format allows you to easily absorb and utilize the information without feeling overwhelmed. I have also shared part of my story to help you see the code at work in real-life situations and the results it produced. I want you to understand how the codes were created and how they can support your efforts and endeavors.

Each *Success Principle, Success Mindset,* and *Success Code* form the three cornerstones of successful living and are more than just a collection of ideas. They are fundamental principles designed to *inspire, enlighten,* and *transform* you. Following the structure and engaging with these principles will equip you with the tools and mindsets needed to navigate your unique path to success.

Each success component reflects a unique aspect of life and how you can use them to achieve success. Through explanation, definition, and sharing of my personal stories, I illustrate the real-world impact of these codes, showing you practical examples of how they have shaped my journey and can inspire yours. I aim to ensure the codes are well-defined and clear so you can use them to map your journey and foster the skills required to reach your full potential.

THE SUCCESS PRINCIPLES

The *Success Principles* are your foundation, providing the essential tools and mindset to achieve your goals and embodying your core values, beliefs, and actions that drive meaningful success. These principles are practical guidelines that you can apply to transform your life. *Success Principles* perpetuate a journey of self-discovery and growth, helping to awaken your purpose by discovering your true calling and aligning your actions with your deepest passions. In this section, you will expand your beliefs, breaking free from the limiting thoughts that have held you back and adopting empowering ones that propel you forward. Living authentically will become your new norm as you embrace your true self and live in accordance with these new *principles*, creating a life of integrity and fulfillment.

Success Principles help you transcend barriers, overcoming obstacles that impede your progress with resilience and determination. They allow you to view failures as opportunities for growth and transformation. By clarifying *your* success principles, you will define what truly matters to you and set clear, achievable objectives. Adopting and embracing the *Success Principles* in your life is essential for unlocking your full potential and achieving lasting fulfillment. These principles act as a compass, guiding you through the complexities of life and helping you stay focused on what truly matters. By integrating these values into your daily routines and decisions, you build a strong foundation for success and a resilience to external challenges and setbacks.

Embracing these principles means committing to continuous growth, self-awareness, and purposeful action. It transforms your mindset from limitation to possibility, enabling you to navigate your journey with confidence, clarity, and a deep sense of purpose.

Within each principle, you'll learn how to:

- **Awaken Purpose -** Discover your true calling and align your actions with your deepest passions.
- **Expand Beliefs -** Break free from limiting beliefs that hold you back and adopt empowering ones.
- **Live Authentically -** Embrace your true self and live in accordance with your values.
- **Transcend Barriers -** Overcome obstacles that impede your progress.
- **Turn Failure into Success -** Learn to see failures as opportunities for growth and transformation.
- **Clarify Values and Goals -** Define what truly matters to you and set clear, achievable goals.

Ultimately, the *Success Principles* empowers you to live a life that is successful by external standards and also deeply satisfying and aligned with your innermost values and aspirations.

THE SUCCESS MINDSET

At its core, a *Success Mindset* is about cultivating the right mental attitude to support your journey toward achieving your goals and realizing your full potential. It's not only about positive thinking; it's a fundamental shift in how you perceive challenges, setbacks, and your own capabilities.

Embracing the *Success Mindset* means developing key mental attributes that will serve as the foundation for your growth and achievement. These include resilience, which allows you to bounce back from setbacks and view obstacles as opportunities for learning; a positive attitude that helps you navigate life's challenges with optimism and constructive energy; a growth orientation that fuels your passion for continuous learning and improvement; and a strong sense of self-worth that builds your confidence and belief in your abilities.

Adopting the *Success Mindset* is not just changing how you think. It's changing how you act and react to the world around you. This mindset empowers you to take control of your personal development, embrace challenges as opportunities for growth, and persist in the face of adversity. Recognize that your abilities and intelligence are not fixed traits. Instead, they are qualities you can develop through dedication and hard work. With this perspective, you'll find yourself more willing to step out of your comfort zone, take calculated risks, and pursue ambitious goals.

Having a *Success Mindset* is the primary shift you will need to make to transform your life, enabling you to achieve your goals and realize your full potential. You'll develop a positive attitude that fuels your optimism and constructive energy and fosters a growth orientation that keeps you passionate about continuous learning and improvement. A strong sense of self-worth will also bolster your confidence and belief in your abilities. This fundamental shift will empower you to take control of your personal development, embrace challenges, and persist in the face of adversity, ultimately leading to a more fulfilling, purposeful, and successful life.

The *Success Mindset* will guide you in developing:

- **Resilience** - Building mental strength to bounce back from setbacks.
- **Positive Attitude** - Fostering an optimistic outlook to navigate life's challenges.
- **Growth Orientation** - Embracing continuous learning and improvement.
- **Self-Worth** - Developing a strong sense of self-esteem and confidence.
- **Confidence** - Deeply knowing and understanding yourself.

THE SUCCESS CODE

The pivotal and profound *Success Codes* encapsulate the essence of the *Success Principles* and a *Success Mindset* into a single, memorable guiding mantra. Each code distills the core values, beliefs, and actions necessary for meaningful success into one succinct sentence or theme. It serves as a powerful touchstone that you can return to repeatedly, reminding you of the foundational truths that drive your journey forward. The *Success Code* becomes your personal compass, simplifying the complexities of success into a clear, actionable, and inspiring guideline.

Committing to each *Success Code* ensures that every decision and action aligns with your core values and creates a cohesive and focused approach to success. The power of each *Success Code* lies in its simplicity and universality. It is easy to remember and apply in various situations, providing a consistent framework for making choices and evaluating progress. Whether facing a significant life decision, a minor setback, or an opportunity for growth, each *Success Code* serves as a reliable North Star and guides you toward actions that reflect your highest ideals. By embracing each code, you cultivate a disciplined and principled approach to life, ensuring that your path to success is effective, deeply fulfilling, and aligned with your true self.

You'll find a powerful *Success Code* at the end of each chapter. Use it as a quick reference point to remind yourself of the core lessons you must implement and make its message your mantra.

EMBRACING THE COMMITMENT

The work you are about to do will channel your ambition into a positive and meaningful purpose that will drive you toward your goals. If you have the desire and the willingness, that's half the battle. Knowing something is one thing; implementing it into your life is another. The only way any of this will impact your life is if you use it consistently and integrate it wholeheartedly into the way you conduct your life. Remember, you are here because you're ready to unlock your full potential and go after your dreams. You want success that feels meaningful and aligns with your values and passions. That makes you unique and puts you at the forefront of harnessing your talents to achieve something great.

This will be a journey of finding your passion and purpose while leveraging your strengths to create a meaningful impact in the world. Some of what you will learn may challenge your current thinking and push you out of your comfort zone. *Welcome it!* I know from experience that you grow when you are stretched beyond your comfort zone. Time and time again, circumstances forced me outside my comfort zone, and those moments defined me. I took a chance on myself, and I succeeded. That mindset of taking ownership of my potential and betting on myself became the foundation of everything I am now eager to teach you.

I know that some of my ideas will hit home immediately, helping you redefine what success looks like for you. Others may feel unconventional or unfamiliar. Like me, you will need to push past limiting beliefs, question old ways of thinking, and decide that you are worth the effort. By learning from my journey and using the *Success Codes* as your compass, you will overcome obstacles and achieve success far quicker than I did. I did not have these principles laid out for me growing up. I had to forge them through trial, failure, and persistence. Now, they are in your hands, ready for you to carry forward.

Each aspect of this process is about breaking away from what society tells you success should look like and instead embracing what feels authentic and fulfilling to you. I want you to use the Codes to hone your perspective and recognize the incredible power already within you. In my opinion, these are not just the key to success; they are the cornerstones of truly living. When you embrace the *Success Code* way of thinking, you will do more than change your own life. You will also inspire those around you and create a ripple effect that transforms communities, industries, and generations to come.

All you have to do is:

- **Live the Success *Principles*:** Be a beacon of success in your life and use the principles as the foundation of what you want to be known for and who you aspire to become.
- **Implement the *Success Mindset*:** Regularly review and reflect on the *Success Mindset*. Integrate this thinking into your daily practices to create lasting change and achieve your goals.
- **Adopt the *Success Codes*:** Embrace the fundamental meaning as part of your daily activities and integrate it into your actions, behaviors, and attitudes. Keep the *Success Codes* handy in a notebook, on your phone, or as part of your daily routine to reinforce the habits and attitudes you are developing.

Remember, this journey isn't just about reaching a destination; it's about embracing the process, learning, growing, and becoming the best version of yourself along the way. You've got this, and I'm here with you every step of the way.

ONE

The Internal Foundation

BUILDING YOUR PERSONAL SUCCESS

The Real Work Begins Within Where You Define
What Success Really Means To You.

Before you can achieve any meaningful success in the world, you must first build a strong foundation within yourself. Success is not just about reaching external goals; it is about aligning your mindset, values, and well-being to create a life that feels fulfilling from the inside out. Too often, we are taught to chase success by focusing on outcomes like titles, salaries, and recognition. But without the internal tools to support those achievements, success can feel hollow, unsustainable, and even overwhelming. The truth is, your external achievements will only ever be as strong as the internal foundation you build to support them.

Look at people like Sophia Amoruso and Brandon Stanton. Their legacies extend far beyond their achievements. Their success wasn't just a product of their talents or opportunities; it was rooted in their *unshakable sense of self, resilience, and an alignment with their core values.*

Sophia Amoruso, founder of Nasty Gal and author of *#GIRLBOSS* has become a symbol of entrepreneurial resilience, showing how authenticity and self-belief can redefine success.

Brandon Stanton, creator of Humans of New York, has built a story-telling movement that highlights the beauty of human resilience. His work echoes Brené Brown's ability to use storytelling to inspire and create connection.

These icons teach us that success isn't just what you achieve; it's who you become in the process. Without a solid internal foundation, external accomplishments are fragile. We've seen many people reach great heights only to struggle with burnout, personal crises, or a loss of purpose because they didn't develop the inner strength to sustain their success.

But here's the most important part: this isn't about them, it's about you. You have the potential to apply these same principles to your own life. You don't need to be a celebrity or a business mogul to create meaningful success. You just need the right mindset, the willingness to adapt, and the courage to stay true to your values.

Whether you're climbing the corporate ladder, launching your own business, or figuring out your next steps in life, the external application of these codes will help you navigate the world with clarity and confidence.

This matters because you deserve a life that feels both successful and fulfilling. It's not enough to achieve goals if they don't align with *who you are.* The world is full of opportunities, but without the tools to recognize and seize them, it's easy to feel stuck, overwhelmed, or disconnected from your true purpose.

APPLY THE CODES IN YOUR LIFE

In this section, we'll explore the essential codes that create this foundation. These are the principles that guide how you think, how you show up for yourself, and how you navigate the inevitable challenges along the way. From redefining what success truly means to prioritizing your well-being, cultivating emotional intelligence, and discovering your deeper purpose, these codes will equip you with the tools needed to create lasting, meaningful success.

As you move through this section, I encourage you to reflect deeply on your current beliefs and habits. *Are they aligned with your values?*

Do they support the life you want to create? This is your opportunity to lay the groundwork for achieving success and becoming the person who can sustain and grow it.

Success doesn't start with what you achieve. It starts with *who you are.* And when you build from a place of authenticity, resilience, and purpose, there's no limit to what you can accomplish.

CHAPTER 1

THE REDEFINING SUCCESS CODE

Success Is About Creating Your Own Definition
Of Fulfillment And Achievement.

W̄e believe, in today's world, that success means checking off a list of achievements as if it were a grocery list. *How often do we find social media posts about someone getting a high academic qualification leading to costly celebrations?* Life encompasses so much more than that. Success should be about finding that sweet spot where personal fulfillment positively impacts society and still enjoying one's life and career path. For the younger generations, success is a mix of mastering the work-life balance, making a difference in the community, and ensuring life has both meaning and purpose. I have learnt that success is a deeply personal journey, not some kind of check the box exercise. Millennials have the unique opportunity to break free from outdated norms, balance work and life meaningfully, and create a definition of success rooted in purpose, impact, and self-awareness.

Young adults often go into jobs that seem satisfying at first, but they soon realize these roles do not align with their values or passions. Many take whatever opportunity comes their way, believing it will be enough, only to feel unfulfilled after a few months. This happens because they are not aware of the broader range of choices available to them. In this book, I teach them how to find careers that offer more than just a paycheck; jobs that bring meaning and purpose to their lives. I have seen many of them jump from job to job, seeking fulfillment yet feeling unfulfilled because they haven't taken the time to understand what truly drives them. My journey, which was filled with early morning sales and the struggle to find my footing, taught me that aligning one's career with personal values and passions is crucial. Through the hardship and triumphs, I realized success is more than just financial gain. It is also about finding joy and meaning in what you do. When you align your work with your core values, you unlock a deeper satisfaction from within.

I want you to know that your value and worth are not defined by your income. True self-worth comes from recognizing your intrinsic qualities, skills, and contributions to the world. It is about understanding that your talents, compassion, and efforts to make a positive impact are what truly matter. Financial success is just one aspect of life, but it does not capture the entirety of your potential and the meaningful ways you can enrich the lives of others and yourself.

Modern trends show that this generation is redefining success in ways that are aligning with their values and aspirations. The rise of the gig economy and digital nomad lifestyles highlights their preference for flexibility and autonomy while the quiet quitting movement reflects a rejection of burnout in favor of meaningful work-life balance.

In the era I grew up in, success was highly valued, and our parents pushed us to do our absolute best. We didn't have the resources available today, and we did our best to meet both their needs and societal expectations. With the tools and technology you have at your fingertips, you are in an outstanding position to achieve success in many areas of life. The real question is, *How much do you want it? How important is it to you? How much are you willing to do to achieve the success that is just waiting for you to enjoy?* Remember, "Success is your birthright!" Use what you can learn to claim it.

My journey started when the alarm clock went off at 5 AM; it was cold and dark. Some mornings, I was so unmotivated to move I was even in tears, wishing I could lie in my warm floor bed a little longer. But, we did not have a choice, as our survival depended on me getting out of bed.

As shared in Origins of the Code, as a ten-year-old Indian boy, my siblings and I had to go out early every morning and sell the Indian samosas that our mum would make. Our life depended on my siblings and me doing this work. If we did not make a sale, we would not have money to buy groceries for our dinner or lunch the next day. I remember times when dinner was just a glass of water or a cup of tea. My stomach would growl with hunger, but I blocked it out of my mind because there was no other option.

There was a mixture of pride and shame when we went out. I noticed the judgment on people's faces when they opened the door to me with my basket of delicacies in hand, ready to be sold. Yet, I was glad to be helping my family. The excitement when making a sale was so fulfilling that it motivated us to venture out the next day. Each sale became a defining moment of success for me, highlighting the value of teamwork as we celebrated together. That experience reinforced that while we were already a close-knit family, working together toward a common goal brought us even closer and emphasized the importance of collaboration in achieving success.

Life was difficult in South Africa, but we were grateful that we had each other. As a young boy, there were days when I went to school with worn-out shoes or without a sweater on cold, rainy mornings. We were subjected to bullying from other children, who would tease and shame us relentlessly. Their constant teasing and ridicule created a deep sense of insecurity and self-doubt within me. Every day at school was a struggle, as their hurtful words and actions chipped away at my confidence. I couldn't escape the constant mockery that made me feel isolated and humiliated. Their bullying affected my self-esteem, had a lasting impact on my emotional well-being, and shaped the way I viewed myself and the world around me.

Now, when I look back on my life, I feel proud that I continued my pursuit of becoming the best version of myself amidst all the obstacles and challenges along the journey. This journey has taught me that true fulfillment comes from continually evolving, learning, and making a positive impact on the lives of others, not just from financial success. I learned that money and income do one thing, but personal growth and self-improvement provide so much more. When we embrace purpose over profit, we discover a deeper sense of happiness that transcends monetary gains. We create a meaningful and impactful life by focusing on what truly matters.

Many millennials think that success is about pushing through challenges, but it is not! It's about recognizing the value of your emotional well-being and striving to create a life that feels balanced and meaningful. Think about it, *how often do you pause and ask yourself, 'Am I thriving, or just surviving?'* Having the courage to seek therapy, set boundaries, and make mindfulness a part of your daily lives is not a weakness, it's strength. Remember, taking care of your mental health lays the foundation for everything else in life. It helps you realise deeper truths about what drives you, what fulfills you, and what truly matters.

My journey selling samosas may have seemed like I was simply sell-ing snacks to make a few extra bucks. However, to me, it was much more than that. Each sale represented a small victory that contributed to my family's survival. That sense of purpose motivated me to get up at 5 AM, braving the cold, dark mornings. Selling samosas was not just about immediate financial gain; it was about ensuring my family had food. This purpose-driven mindset made every sale sig-nificant and fulfilling. It instilled in me the importance of aligning my efforts with a deeper meaning, which became a guiding principle throughout my life.

SUCCESS PRINCIPLE

Redefining Success means you must not perceive success merely as advancing in the corporate hierarchy or gathering wealth. Think about purpose-driven endeavors where you are seeking meaning in what you are doing while feeling rewarded for what you accomplish. Often, we prioritize job satisfaction but overlook the importance of aligning our careers with our values and passions. True satisfaction comes from doing something that resonates with your core values. When you align your work with what truly matters to you, you discover a deeper level of satisfaction and purpose. It's not just about the paycheck; it's about doing something that fulfills you and positively impacts the world.

SUCCESS MINDSET

In pursuing purposeful endeavors, prioritize roles and opportunities that align with your values. Seek careers that reflect your beliefs, allowing them to be effective and contribute positively to the causes you care about. This alignment fosters a sense of fulfillment and motivation in your professional journey.

Ultimately, embracing purpose over profit signifies a shift toward holistic success. As a millennial, you will recognize that success encompasses more than just financial achievements; it is about finding fulfillment, making a difference, and leaving a positive legacy. It is about aligning personal goals with a broader sense of purpose and social responsibility.

1. **Follow Your Passion**
   - You have to choose careers or opportunities that excite you and match your interests. Doing what you love makes your journey more rewarding and boosts your drive to excel.

2. **Make a Positive Impact**
   - Think about solutions that can benefit your community. Whether through business, community work, or personal projects, aim to leave the world better than you found it.

3. **Measure Success Beyond Money**
   - You must always remember that true success is not just about earning money. It is also about achieving personal growth, helping others, and most importantly, finding meaning in what you do.

SUCCESS CODE: **PERSONAL VALUES**

Find purpose and passion in what you do. Align with your values and put personal enrichment over profit gain.

CHAPTER 2

THE PURPOSE-MINDED CODE

Set yourself up for a life of joy and fulfillment by
being on purpose every day.

Imagine turning ordinary thoughts into powerful actions that bring meaning to your life and positively impact the world around you. That's what purpose-minded means. It is more than just setting goals or achieving personal success; it is about understanding the deeper 'why' behind your actions and aligning your efforts with a meaningful outcome. Purpose-minded is the difference between chasing superficial achievements versus striving for something that brings fulfillment and greater impact. When a clear purpose guides our ambitions, we can channel our energy into pursuits that benefit ourselves and also contribute to the collective good.

Unlike previous generations that have primarily focused on monetary accomplishments, your generation is more inclined toward finding fulfillment internally. As change makers, your experiences and contributions resonate with your personal needs rather than conforming to conventional markers of success.

The great news is that purpose does not need to be confined to a single idea. Some find their '*why*' in the creative process, while others find it in parenting, volunteering, or championing a cause they care about deeply. It is important to recognize that success is not one-size-fits-all. We each walk unique paths, but what unites us is the pursuit of fulfillment. Whether you are revolutionizing industries or simply being present for your family, the purpose is about alignment and living in a way that reflects who you truly are and what you value.

In studying millennials, I have noticed that this generation values authenticity and strives for a sense of purpose in all aspects of their lives. A purposeful life often requires an emotional journey, confronting societal expectations and redefining success on one's own terms. Purpose-minded means understanding that 'holistic' success is not just about financial achievements or societal status and is instead about finding joy and satisfaction in a pursuit that resonates with one's personal desires and passions throughout life.

For me, the journey to purpose has been one of discovery through both triumph and struggle. Growing up, entrepreneurship was never on the radar. The script was simple: *go to school, get a stable job, get married and provide for your family.* Success was defined by security, not by chasing bold ideas. For years, I worked in corporate environments that felt disconnected from the idea of purpose. The daily grind, deadlines, and constant pressure often left little room for reflection or meaning. Yet, even in those moments, I found myself drawn to opportunities where I could create a difference, even in small ways. I remember organizing feeding programs over the weekends and coordinating efforts to bring meals to those in need. It started as a small initiative, a way to give back amidst the chaos, but it planted a seed of purpose within me.

As I grew in my career, I realized that my purpose did not just lie in achieving professional milestones; it came alive when I helped others grow. Mentoring my colleagues became a natural extension of who I was. Watching them climb the ladder, build confidence, and achieve their goals gave me more satisfaction than any corporate recognition ever could. Each conversation and each shared piece of advice felt like a small ripple of impact that extended far beyond me.

Over time, my desire to empower others went beyond the walls of the corporate world. Mentoring the youth became my way of planting seeds for the future. I saw the potential in these young minds, and guiding them helped me realize that purpose isn't always self-serving. It's about contributing to others.

Today, I live purposefully through initiatives close to my heart. From supporting people with disabilities to leading projects that bridge gaps in society, I have found meaning in serving. I align each venture, whether climbing Kilimanjaro to raise awareness or helping build sustainable communities, with my core belief that purpose is found not in grand gestures, rather in the small, consistent actions that uplift others. My journey has taught me that purpose is not a destination or a title. It is a way of life that is shaped by the choices we make daily to live meaningfully and serve the greater good.

Purpose does not come from following the script, it emerges from finding purpose in unexpected places. Not everyone can abandon their responsibilities to pursue their passions. Instead, we can enjoy what I call 'micro-purpose' by injecting meaning into even the most routine activities. Whether it's connecting with a colleague, offering mentorship, or finding joy in a creative hobby, these small, intentional moments can transform how we experience life.

The impact we can make by adopting a mindset of micro-purpose-driven principles is profound, both emotionally and psychologically. Such an alignment increases feelings of worthiness and contribution that can arise from pursuing goals that foster personal significance. Emotionally, purpose fosters positivity and motivation, as you are driven by doing things that transcend monetary rewards. It also cultivates a sense of community and belonging, as you often seek like-minded individuals and organizations that share your values, enhancing your overall well-being and satisfaction with life.

In today's fast-paced and hyper-connected world, finding purpose can seem like an elusive goal. However, your generation has access to unique opportunities that can align your passions with your daily lives. One powerful way to do this is by infusing meaning into your work. Even if your job is not your dream role, you can still create purpose initiatives. Often, you can find purpose in smaller, everyday acts. Helping a coworker succeed or solving a problem that benefits others can be incredibly rewarding.

Beyond work, purpose can manifest in how you spend your time and energy outside the office. Volunteering for causes close to your heart, whether it's tutoring students, taking part in food distribution, or environmental clean-ups, allows you to make a direct impact. Creative hobbies like painting, writing, or music are also meaningful outlets that bring personal joy and inspire others.

As digital gurus, you can also harness technology to live more purposefully. Social media offers a platform to advocate for causes, build communities, and inspire action on a global scale. Crowd-funding platforms enable individuals to support or launch impactful projects. Digital side hustles such as blogs, online businesses, or podcasts provide ways to align your personal passions with creating value for others.

Global trends have also opened new pathways for purpose-driven living. Many millennials are embracing sustainability practices, such as reducing waste and supporting ethical brands, as part of their lifestyle. The rise of remote work allows individuals to explore the world while engaging in meaningful cultural exchanges.

Remember, purpose isn't a one-size-fits-all concept; it's a multifaceted journey woven into life's various aspects. A software engineer might find fulfillment in designing tools that improve access to education, while a fitness enthusiast could inspire others by sharing their health journey online. A corporate employee might dedicate their weekends to organizing charity fundraisers. Purpose does not require grand gestures. It starts with small, intentional actions that create a ripple effect.

The essence of a fulfilling life lies in living with purpose. It's about approaching each day with intentionality, consciously aligning your goals with your deeply held values, and taking inspired action toward them. By doing so, you infuse every experience with meaning and significance.

SUCCESS PRINCIPLE

Purpose Minded – Being purpose-minded is not about abandoning responsibility in pursuit of passion; it is about intentionally infusing purpose into every aspect of your life. Titles, financial gain, or external validation do not measure true success, but it can be measured by the depth of meaning and fulfillment you create through your daily actions. This success principle emphasizes that purpose is not merely a term, rather it is a way of living. You find it in the small, intentional choices you make each day and in how you show up, contribute, and align your ambitions with what truly matters to you.

To embody this principle, start by redefining success on your own terms. Move beyond traditional benchmarks and ask yourself: *What impact do I want to have? What kind of energy do I want to bring into the world?* Purpose-minded individuals do not just seek achievement, they seek alignment between their values and their actions.

Success in this context is about cultivating *micro-purpose* and finding meaning even in routine tasks, whether it is mentoring a colleague, supporting a cause, or using creativity to inspire others—it is about realizing that purpose is not always about changing the world in one sweeping act. It's more so about the consistent, intentional ways you uplift others and stay connected to what lights you up.

This principle also highlights the importance of adaptability. As your purpose evolves, so will your path. Be willing to reflect, recalibrate, and embrace the unexpected opportunities that align with your core values. Surround yourself with a community that fosters growth and shares your vision. Seek mentorship, engage in purpose-driven initiatives, and allow your journey to be shaped by experiences that deepen your sense of meaning. As you develop a purpose-minded mindset, it is increasingly important to align your ambitions with your core values and understand that genuine success stems from a deep sense of purpose and commitment.

Here are some success principles designed to help you live a more purposeful life:

1. Align Your Ambitions with Your Core Values
  - Aligning your ambitions with your core values means choosing goals and careers that reflect who you truly are and what you believe in. Find meaning in what you do and make sure your work resonates with your personal principles.
  - Reflect on what matters most to you. *What are your values and passions?* Once you know these, look for opportunities and roles that align with them.

2. Seek Personal Fulfillment and Social Impact

- True fulfillment comes from doing work that is personally meaningful and makes a positive impact on the world.
- Look for roles that advance your career while also contributing to something greater.

3. Engage in Self-Discovery and Intentional Decision-Making

- Understanding your passions and values helps you make decisions that align with your true self. Having this self-awareness leads to more deliberate choices about your career and personal life.
- Practice introspection. Ask yourself what excites you, what you care about, and how you want to make a difference. Use these insights to guide your career choices and personal goals.

4. Set Value-Driven Goals

- Establish goals that mirror your values and make sure you are directing your efforts toward what truly matters to you.
- After identifying your values, set specific and actionable goals that align with them. Make sure these goals guide your daily actions.

5. Create Supportive Environments

- Surround yourself with supportive environments such as purpose-driven organizations or communities that share your values. They can enhance your motivation and resilience.

- Seek workplaces, groups, or networks that align with your values and ambitions. Join communities or organizations that share your goals and build relationships with people who inspire and support you. If such environments are not readily available, consider creating your own or advocating for changes in existing ones.

6. Measure Success by Impact and Fulfillment

- Focusing on the impact you make and the fulfillment you experience provides a more holistic and meaningful view of success.

- Regularly assess how your actions and career align with your values and contribute to a greater good. Reflect on the impact you're making in your community or industry and how fulfilled you feel in your work and life. Use this reflection to guide future decisions and adjust your goals as needed.

SUCCESS MINDSET

As millennials, embracing a thriving mindset that aligns with your purpose-minded approach is essential. This mindset begins with recognizing that true success isn't just about financial milestones or societal recognition, it's about pursuing what truly fulfills you. It's about crafting a life centered on what inspires, energizes, and empowers you.

Start by identifying your core values and deepest passions, those elements that spark your enthusiasm and infuse your life with meaning. When you define success on your own terms, you gain clarity, motivation, and a deeper sense of direction. You stop measuring yourself by outdated standards and start making decisions that match your values and long-term vision. This approach not only improves your personal well-being but also impacts the people and communities around you.

Here are three ways you can incorporate a purpose-minded mindset into your life:

1. **Align your goals with your values**
   - Take a step back and identify what truly matters to you. When your ambitions reflect your core beliefs, success becomes more meaningful and fulfilling. Instead of chasing what looks good on paper, focus on what actually excites and motivates you. The more your goals mirror who you are, the easier it becomes to stay committed and push through challenges.

2. Look for ways to create impact

- Purpose is not just about personal success, it's about how you contribute to the world around you. Whether through your work, relationships, or community, find ways to make a difference. This does not always have to be on a massive scale. Small, consistent actions can have a ripple effect. When you shift from just achieving for yourself to creating value for others, your sense of fulfillment deepens.

3. Stay adaptable and open to growth

- Purpose evolves over time. Be willing to reflect, adjust, and embrace new opportunities that are stepping stones toward your bigger vision. The path you start on may not be the one you stay on, and *that is okay.* Growth comes from learning, trying new things, and allowing yourself to pivot when something no longer feels right. The more you evolve, the clearer your purpose becomes.

By embracing a purpose-minded mindset, you are not just aiming for traditional success. You are crafting a life that is rich in meaning, impact, and personal fulfillment. Living a purpose-driven life equips you with resilience and a deeper understanding of what truly matters. It's the foundation for navigating challenges, staying grounded, and finding joy in the journey. Remember, purpose emerges in the relationships you build, the kindness you share, and the difference you make in your immediate environment. Be intentional about aligning your daily actions with your purpose-driven desires for humanity.

If you struggle to uncover your purpose-minded ambitions or are unsure if the work you are pursuing truly aligns with your deeper mission, you're not alone. Finding clarity in a world full of distractions can be challenging, but I am here to help guide you on this journey. I invite you to reach out to me directly via my contact details in the resources page, so that together we can explore what drives you at your core, uncover your passions, and identify the ambitions that will lead to a more meaningful and impactful life. If you're ready to discover a path that resonates with your true purpose, I am happy to work together to unlock the potential within you and create a life that achieves success and leaves a lasting legacy.

SUCCESS CODE: **FINDING PURPOSE**

Purpose is not found in a single leap but in the small, intentional steps you take every day.

CHAPTER 3

THE MISSION-DRIVEN CODE

Aligning Your Goals With Your Deeper Purpose
Fuels Unstoppable Motivation.

Imagine turning everyday thoughts into actions that not only define your personal success but also leave a lasting impact on the world around you. This is the essence of the mission-driven code, a mindset that transforms the pursuit of success into a journey of meaning, fulfillment, and contribution. In a world often fixated on accolades and achievements, a mission-driven approach challenges us to dig deeper, uncover our 'why,' and align our goals in a direction that resonates with our core values. Mission-driven is about shifting from chasing success to building a life that matters genuinely.

Unlike previous generations that may have prioritized financial security or traditional career milestones, millennials are redefining success on their own terms. You value authenticity and alignment, seeking careers and lifestyles that reflect your passions and beliefs. Whether it's advocating for social justice, embracing innovative ways to solve pressing global challenges, or simply creating work that has emotional and social resonance, a desire to make a meaningful difference fuels your ambitions. The mission-driven code celebrates your commitment to prioritizing your goals and explores how you can cultivate ambitions that align with both personal growth and broader societal impact.

The journey toward fulfilling your mission-driven ambitions is going to be filled with both excitement and challenges. Being on a mission requires you to confront societal norms, reimagine traditional definitions of success, and take bold steps toward living a life that feels both authentic and impactful. Through self-reflection, value-aligned goal setting, and surrounding yourself with a community that shares your vision, you can embrace a mission-driven journey with clarity and courage. The rewards once achieved go beyond material success. They offer emotional fulfillment and a deeper connection to the world around you.

Going after your mission means also aligning with your purpose and turning those two things into a powerful force that shapes your ambitions and the legacy you leave behind.

Allow me to share about my mission on the mountain. One of the most profound experiences that shaped my understanding of mission-driven ambitions was climbing Mount Kilimanjaro, the highest mountain in Africa, to raise awareness and funds for our *Skills Village*, along with our cancer and mental wellness initiatives. Over twelve weeks, *the Skills Village* focuses on preparing youth mentally to learn vocational skills, including electrical and mechanical work. With this methodology, we create employment for them, allowing them to feed their families. The concept of teaching someone to fish. The journey was not just about reaching the summit; it was a mission to create lasting impact and support causes that deeply resonate with my purpose. From the moment I conceived the idea, I knew that the project required more than just physical preparation. It needed a mission-driven mindset, unwavering commitment, and a team that shared the same vision.

The first challenge was assembling the right team, a group of individuals who believed in the mission and were wholeheartedly committed to achieving it. I presented three clear goals: raising funds to establish and support our *Skills Village* initiative, driving awareness and support for cancer-related causes, and advocating for mental wellness on a broader scale. Once the team understood the purpose behind our mission, we divided the work into manageable tasks, and each member contributed their unique skills, from training for the climb to organizing fundraising events and ensuring we had the right equipment. Every step was intentional and aligned with our shared vision and end results.

To maintain our focus and drive, we created a daily intention statement, reminding ourselves of the impact we wanted to create. Visualization became a cornerstone of our preparation. I encouraged the team to imagine us standing together at the summit, celebrating our victory, and feeling the fulfillment of accomplishing something greater than ourselves. This emotional connection to the goal fueled our actions, and I am proud to say that we achieved everything we set out to do. We pushed ourselves even further by hosting the first-ever Shavathon at the summit, where I shaved my hair along with other team members. The standard guideline that climbers should stay at the summit of Mount Kilimanjaro for a minimum of fifteen minutes is not an official rule but rather a commonly followed practice advised by experienced guides and trekking companies. This is due to extreme altitude, low oxygen levels, and the risk of altitude sickness. However, there is no single person or authority credited with setting this exact timeframe, it is based on altitude safety recommendations and practical experience from high-altitude trekkers and mountaineering experts. Despite this, we remained at the summit for about thirty minutes, embracing the moment and the significance of our mission.

That entire experience taught me that mission-driven ambitions are about more than just achieving goals. They are about aligning your actions with a purpose that resonates deeply within you. Purpose-infused goals transform every challenge into a growth opportunity, make every step forward meaningful, and create results that extend far beyond personal success. This is the mindset I now teach and coach, helping others uncover their own mission-driven ambitions to lead lives of significance, fulfillment, and collective contribution.

For millennials, going through career transitions and aligning ambitions with purpose can feel daunting, yet deeply rewarding. Many are re-evaluating traditional career paths and seeking roles that resonate with their personal values and passions. Consider the example of a corporate lawyer who left a high-paying job to create a non-profit advocating for policy change. They took a leap that required courage and clarity toward a more meaningful mission in their life.

In my life, when I should have been following the traditional career path based on money or accolades, I chose to focus on being mission-driven instead. That led to hours on end of learning a new craft, mastering different skills, and believing in the mission I set out to achieve. It also led to hours of fulfillment, greater connections with others, and the measurable impact I have made in the lives of my community and family members. My mission became my work and my passion. Being on a mission is far more rewarding than any corporate title or company award I might receive.

To follow a similar path in your life, begin by assessing your core values, exploring industries or roles that align with them, and connecting deeply with what matters most to you. Mission-driven ambitions may demand initial sacrifices, but they often lead to greater enjoyment as you contribute meaningfully in areas and industries that resonate more authentically with you.

Recognizing that your mission will evolve over time can free you from the pressure of perfection and allow you to adjust your goals as you grow. Sustaining motivation along your journey involves embracing adaptability and learning from setbacks. Millennials excel in leveraging technology to amplify their ambitions, whether by building online platforms, using social media to connect with like-minded individuals, or crowdfunding for innovative projects. Utilizing unique strategies, not only motivates your drive; it also enables you to leave a lasting legacy of impact and inspiration for others who are learning from you.

As you develop and carry out your mission, avoid burnout or disillusionment, especially when results do not materialize as quickly as expected. It's crucial to maintain a balance between ambition and self-care. Establish realistic milestones, practice mindfulness to reconnect during challenging times, and celebrate small victories along the way. Your mission may take you a week, a year, or even a lifetime. However long you are in pursuit of your mission-driven ambitions, allow them to enrich your life and those around you. A mission of great value is one that enhances who we are and the legacy we desire to manifest.

SUCCESS PRINCIPLE

Mission-Driven success is defined by aligning your goals with your core values and pursuing a life of fulfillment and meaningful impact. This principle challenges the traditional markers of success, such as wealth or status, and encourages you to seek a path that resonates deeply with your personal values and aspirations. By embracing a mission-driven mindset, you empower yourself to focus on goals that not only advance you financially but also enhance your well-being, contribute to your community, and reflect your authentic self. When success is no longer a destination measured in numbers, it becomes a journey enriched by purposeful experiences and alignment with what truly matters.

Embracing mission-driven ambitions requires intentional action and self-discovery. Engage in reflective practices like self-reflection, journaling, mindfulness, or mentorship to uncover your true passions. Use these ways of obtaining clarity to set goals that resonate with your highest values, and immerse yourself in environments that foster shared purpose, such as like-minded communities or purpose-focused organizations. By committing to this principle of being mission-driven, you focus on and feel the satisfaction of creating a life of authenticity and impact. Ask any of the greatest and most successful people in the world, and they will agree that mission-driven ambitions provide a foundation for lifelong fulfillment.

SUCCESS MINDSET

Adopting a *Success Mindset* rooted in mission-driven ambitions is more than a choice. It is a transformative approach to living authentically and meaningfully. True success goes beyond financial gains or social status; it lies in pursuing what genuinely matters to you. Understanding your core values and passions will bring enthusiasm and purpose to your life. You can then create a foundation for aligning your goals with your deeper self for even greater fulfillment.

Combine self-reflection and deliberate steps to define goals that advance your career, personal growth, and societal good. Embrace your ambitions, and as you navigate the journey before you, recognize that *success is as much about the path as it is about the destination.* Surround yourself with a supportive community that shares your vision, offers encouragement, and inspires you along the way. By weaving these principles into your daily life, you will live a fulfilling, mission-driven existence, where your ambitions harmonize with your core essence and make a positive impact on the world.

Here are six steps you can follow to align your mindset with this transformative principle of being mission-driven:

1. **Conduct a Purpose Audit**
   - Take time to reflect on your passions and values. List activities that energize you, bring meaning to your life, and reflect your deepest beliefs. Use this exercise to identify your core motivators and clarify the 'why' behind your ambitions.

2. **Set Value-Driven Goals**
   - Create goals that mirror your purpose rather than external expectations. Ensure your ambitions encompass career success, personal fulfillment, and social impact. Break these goals into actionable steps, keeping your values at the forefront.

3. **Practice Self-Reflection**
   - Dedicate time regularly to self-reflection. Assess whether your actions align with your mission and adjust your trajectory as needed. This practice keeps you grounded and focused on what truly matters to you.

4. **Cultivate Focus and Adaptability**
   - Understand that setbacks and challenges are a natural part of pursuing mission-driven ambitions. Cultivate a focused mindset by embracing all moments as opportunities for growth. Learn to adapt while staying committed to your mission.

5. **Build a Supportive Community**
   - Surround yourself with like-minded individuals who share your vision or inspire you to grow. A supportive network fosters accountability, offers encouragement, and provides a sounding board for ideas, ensuring you stay aligned with your mission.

6. **Celebrate the Journey**
   - Recognize that success is not just about achieving goals, it is also about the growth and fulfillment you experience along the way. Celebrate and highlight milestones at every step of the process, and appreciate the lessons learned along the way.

When we look at any outstanding achievements, be it the invention of the lightbulb, flying the first airplane, formulating penicillin, cloning a sheep, or wanting to inhabit Mars, they all begin with one person deciding that goal was *their* mission. They were going to be the ones to chart the way, no matter what it took. Millennials have made many of the greatest inventions, discoveries, and heralded accomplishments. Their desires, focus, and fortitude kept them mission-driven, and the world is a better place because of their mission-driven success code.

SUCCESS CODE: **MISSION DRIVEN**

*Align your mission with purpose,
and success will follow in fulfillment,
impact, and authenticity.*

CHAPTER 4

THE EMOTIONAL INTELLIGENCE CODE

Awareness And Emotional Mastery Lead To Better Decisions

And Stronger Relationships.

W hen people hear 'mindfulness' and 'emotional intelligence,' they often assume they're just buzzwords; however, I see them as life-altering practices fundamental to true success. Growing up, I was not exposed to any tools that promoted mental, physical, and emotional balance, and like many, I fell into the trap of prioritizing work and external achievements over well-being. But everything changed in my thirties when I discovered holistic meditation, a practice that taught me to integrate mindfulness into my daily life. This shift was difficult but transformative. It enabled me to take on challenges like being diagnosed with COVID-19 pneumonia and climbing Mount Kilimanjaro multiple times with resilience, clarity, and strength.

Mindfulness cultivates presence, grounding, and intentionality in our actions, whereas emotional intelligence fosters deeper self and interpersonal connections. Together, they help us lead balanced lives where we can focus on what truly matters. Whether it's setting boundaries, reconnecting with our inner purpose, or simply taking a moment to breathe amidst the chaos, these practices are fulfilling.

This chapter is an invitation for you to reflect on how often you sacrifice your well-being in pursuit of external success. It's a reminder to reframe self-care not as a luxury, rather as a fundamental part of your strategy for a fulfilling life. Consider how harmonizing your passions with your purpose can take this foundation to the next level and help you create a life that feels both successful and deeply meaningful.

Let me take you back to a defining moment in my life, a night when everything seemed tiresome, yet something extraordinary happened. I was working a night shift, packing and sweeping, lost in the rhythm of routine. Stress, fatigue, and the feeling of going through the motions scattered and weighed down my mind. And then, out of nowhere, I heard a voice. It was not audible to anyone else, but it was unmistakable to me.

"Is this where you want to be? Packing and sweeping for the rest of your life?"

That question hit me like a bolt of lightning. It was not just a fleeting thought; it was the universe urging me to wake up. For the first time in a long while, I stopped… I reflected… I realized how disconnected I had been, not just from my purpose but from myself. I had been living on autopilot, pushing through exhaustion and ignoring the emotional toll of it all.

My mindfulness journey started at that moment. I started by taking small steps, pausing to breathe, reflecting on my values, and seeking practices that would ground me. With time, I found a lifeline in holistic meditation. These techniques helped me manage my stress, find clarity, and reconnect with my emotional core. Because of them, I could face challenges head-on.

Through mindfulness, I did not just find balance; I found the resilience of tackling life's biggest obstacles while building deeper, more meaningful connections with those around me. It taught me that real success is not about how much one can endure or achieve in isolation. It is about how present, connected, and intentional you are in your life's journey.

Emotional intelligence and mindfulness offer a different approach when it comes to success. Instead of chasing external validation, they help you develop self-awareness, manage stress, and create meaningful connections. Mindfulness is not just about meditation. It is about being present in your own life, recognizing when you are running on empty, and making choices that resonate with your well-being. Emotional intelligence strengthens your ability to navigate challenges with grace, whether it is handling a difficult boss, maintaining relationships in a digital world, or setting boundaries with toxic influences.

True success is not about how much you can endure. It is about how well you manage your energy, emotions, and mental clarity. When you integrate mindfulness into your daily routine, you shift from reacting to responding, from burnout to balance, and from comparison to self-confidence. This is not just about feeling better. It is about showing up as your best self in every area of your life.

SUCCESS PRINCIPLE

Mindfulness and Emotional Intelligence are not just about achieving goals or reaching milestones. They are about how you navigate the journey. Balance, achieved through mindfulness and emotional intelligence, is the key to realising your full potential. When you take time to quiet the noise around you, you gain clarity of thought and purpose, making it easier to prioritize what truly matters. Emotional intelligence helps you build stronger relationships by fostering empathy and effective communication, transforming connections into partnerships that uplift and inspire.

Balance is about doing what aligns with your values and goals, rather than simply doing it all. By integrating mindfulness into your daily routine, you can manage stress, prevent burnout, and approach challenges with a calm and focused mind. Emotional intelligence allows you to respond thoughtfully to setbacks and turn obstacles into opportunities for growth. A significant personal challenge involved a thirteen-day stay in the intensive care unit; however, I emerged stronger and subsequently published my first book, a true example of turning pain into a success story. The tools below will enable you to navigate life's complexities with resilience and grace, fueling a brilliance that shines through your personal and professional endeavors.

SUCCESS MINDSET

Approach each day, understanding that genuine success begins internally. Cultivate the mindset that your thoughts, emotions, and actions must align with your inner peace and core values. Instead of allowing external pressures to dictate your journey, take charge of your narrative by practicing mindfulness and nurturing emotional intelligence. Embrace challenges as opportunities to learn and grow, allowing balance and self-awareness to guide your decisions.

Leading from within means prioritizing well-being to enhance clarity, resilience, and genuine connections. This mindset shifts your focus from simply achieving to thriving, enabling you to create a life of purpose and fulfillment while inspiring others to do the same.

1. **Self-Awareness Exercises**
   - **Daily Reflection Journal:** Spend five to ten minutes each evening writing about your emotions during the day. *What triggered them, and how did you react?* Over time, this practice will help you to identify patterns in your behavior and increase your awareness of emotional triggers.
   - **Body Check-In:** Pause during the day to notice where you are holding tension in your body. Stress often manifests physically in tight shoulders, a clenched jaw, or shallow breathing. By identifying these signs, you can address emotional distress before it escalates.

2. **Empathy-Building Practices**

 · **Active Listening:** Practice fully focusing on the person speaking, resisting the urge to interject or formulate your response while they are talking. Reflect back what you've heard to confirm understanding by saying things like, "What I'm hearing is..."

 · **Perspective-Taking:** When disagreements arise, intentionally consider the situation from the other person's viewpoint. Ask yourself, *"What might they be feeling or experiencing that's influencing their actions?"*

3. **Conflict Resolution Techniques**

 · **Pause and Process:** When conflict arises, take a moment before responding to calm your emotions. Deep breathing exercises, such as inhaling for four counts, holding for four, and exhaling for six, can help restore clarity.

 · **Collaborative Problem-Solving:** Approach disagreements with curiosity rather than defensiveness. Use statements like, "Let's work together to find a solution,and focus on the shared goal rather than assigning blame."

4. **Emotion Regulation Strategies**

   · **Name It to Tame It:** When overwhelmed by emotions, label what you are feeling: anger, frustration, sadness, etc. This simple act helps reduce the intensity of the emotion and fosters self-control.

   · **Reframing Negative Thoughts:** Challenge negative self-talk by asking yourself, *Is this thought helpful or accurate?* Replace it with a constructive perspective, such as focusing on what you can control.

5. **Mindfulness for Emotional Intelligence**

   · **Meditation for Emotional Clarity:** Practice mindfulness meditation by sitting quietly, focusing on your breath, and observing your thoughts without judgment. This helps increase your ability to respond thoughtfully rather than react impulsively.

   · **Gratitude Practice:** At the end of each day, list three things you are grateful for. It could be you are grateful for the meals you had today, the connections you made, or just simply for the electricity you have. Gratitude fosters positive emotions, which can improve relationships and emotional resilience.

SUCCESS CODE: **INNER MASTERY**

True success is built from within.
Nurture your mind, master your emotions,
and lead with purpose.

CHAPTER 5

THE HOLISTIC WELL-BEING CODE

Your Physical, Mental, And Emotional Health
Are The Foundation Of Your Success.

G rowing up, the circumstances I found myself in deprived me of access to valuable knowledge and practices regarding *holistic well-being*. A lack of exposure to methods that promote mental, physical, and emotional balance marked my early years. It wasn't until I reached my thirties that I stumbled upon holistic meditation techniques, and they've since become a cornerstone of my daily routine. These practices have profoundly transformed my life, helping me to achieve a sense of peace and balance. By integrating these techniques into my everyday activities, I have been able to manage stress more effectively, enhance my focus, and cultivate a deeper connection with myself and the world around me. My journey into *holistic well-being* has improved my mental clarity and emotional stability and inspired me to share these practices with others, contributing to their journeys toward a more balanced and fulfilling life.

Often, in our younger years, we feel fit, healthy, and strong and are rarely concerned with our overall well-being. We assume our bodies can handle whatever life throws our way, and we don't make the connection between our physical health and other aspects of our lives. This disconnect can lead us down paths that may seem harmless at first, gradually undermining our ability to achieve lasting success and fulfillment.

Many of us fall into patterns of neglecting our health in favor of pursuing career goals, social activities, or other immediate gratifications. We might skip meals, ignore exercise, sacrifice sleep, or adopt unhealthy coping mechanisms to manage stress. These habits, though they may seem manageable in the short term, accumulate and can lead to significant consequences down the road.

Recognizing that your physical health directly impacts your cognitive abilities, emotional stability, and even your financial decision-making is essential. Your body and mind are not separate, they work together to shape your success. Holistic wellness is not just important; it is the foundation of your overall well-being and achievement. When you take care of yourself physically, mentally, and emotionally, you create the energy, focus, and resilience needed to excel in every area of your life.

Throughout my journey of success, I've learned that taking care of my mind, body, and spirit gave me the strength to face my biggest obstacles. This mindset was vital as I went through pneumonia due to COVID-19 and pushed myself to climb Mount Kilimanjaro multiple times. When I focused on my emotional well-being, I was able to realign my priorities, focus on my goals, and fortify my mind with an attitude that served me. I started to exercise again and, with proper nutrition, was able to have the stamina to tackle multiple projects while maintaining focus and enthusiasm.

Reflecting on this, I realize how pivotal the discovery of holistic techniques has been in reshaping my life. The journey has not been easy, but it has been profoundly rewarding. Before this, my life was often marked by stress, confusion, and a sense of being ungrounded. The holistic approach to well-being taught me to address my health from a comprehensive perspective, integrating mind, body, and soul.

For me, success has never been just about strategy, mindset, or financial growth. It has always been about the whole person. I learned early on that my physical, mental, and emotional well-being directly influenced my ability to think clearly, make strong decisions, and stay resilient in the face of challenges. Prioritizing my health improved my focus, energy, and ability to persevere.

Consider this: *How often do you prioritize your work over your well-being? How frequently do you push through fatigue, thinking that success requires constant hustle and sacrifice?* These thought patterns, while common, are counterproductive.

Think about how often you might have said to yourself *I'll sleep when I get old* or *I can handle the stress, it's part of the job.* These statements reflect a mindset that undervalues holistic health's critical role in our overall success.

To change this, you need to reframe your thinking. Instead of viewing self-care as a luxury or an afterthought, you must see it as a fundamental part of your success strategy. Here are some specific statistics and references regarding the overall lack of holistic health among millennials:

- **Mental Health:** According to a report by the American Psychological Association,[1] millennials report higher levels of stress compared to older generations, with 12 percent saying their mental health is 'fair' or 'poor.'[1]
- **Physical Health:** A study published in the Journal of the American Medical Association found that millennials have higher rates of obesity, hypertension, and diabetes compared to previous generations at the same age.[2]
- **Nutrition:** Research from the Centers for Disease Control and Prevention (CDC) shows that only one in ten millennials eat enough fruits and vegetables each day, contributing to poor overall nutrition.[3]

- **Sleep:** The National Sleep Foundation reports that millennials are the most sleep-deprived generation, with 58 percent experiencing symptoms of insomnia at least a few nights per week.[4]
- **Exercise:** Data from the Physical Activity Council indicates that only 22.9 percent of millennials engage in regular physical activity, falling short of recommended exercise guidelines.[5]

As a millennial, you are navigating a fast-paced and constantly changing world. The demands on your time and energy are high, but you can create a balanced and sustainable path to success by prioritizing *holistic well-being*. Embrace a routine that supports all dimensions of your health, and you'll find that your capacity to achieve your goals and maintain long-term happiness will significantly increase. Remember, true success is not just about reaching milestones, but also about enjoying the journey and maintaining a healthy, fulfilling lifestyle.

CONSIDERING CREATING BALANCE AND SUCCESS IN ALL THESE AREAS:

- **Physical health** focuses on maintaining a healthy body through regular exercise, proper nutrition, adequate sleep, and overall physical fitness. It involves taking care of one's body to support vitality and well-being. When I am inspiring my clients, I always make a point of saying, "Treat your body like a temple, and it will serve you longer."

· **Mental and emotional well-being** is about managing stress, coping with emotions, fostering resilience, and maintaining a positive mindset. It involves practices like mindfulness meditation, deep breathing exercises, journaling, daily gratitude practices, setting boundaries, and self-compassion. Giving attention to your internal thoughts and way of feeling will enhance your mental clarity, emotional stability, and psychological resilience.

· **Building and nurturing meaningful relationships** and social connections is not just beneficial but essential for your overall well-being. Human beings are inherently social creatures, and the quality of our relationships significantly impacts our mental and emotional health. It's about more than just having people around us; it's about fostering deep, meaningful connections with family, friends, and communities.

· Spiritual wellness encompasses a deep exploration of your inner world, values, beliefs, and connection to something greater than yourself. At its core, spiritual wellness involves seeking meaning, purpose, and fulfillment in life, often through practices that promote inner peace, reflection, and self-discovery. You will learn more about the journey of self-exploration and introspection when you start to discover and uncover your core values, beliefs, and the principles that guide your life.

- **Occupational wellness** is all about deriving satisfaction and fulfillment from your career choice or profession, harmonizing professional ambitions with personal values and interests. It revolves around achieving a sense of purpose and accomplishment in the workplace, where you feel aligned with your career goals and values. This wellness dimension entails finding meaning in your work, maintaining a healthy work-life balance, nurturing professional growth, and fostering a positive and supportive work environment.

- **Environmental awareness** consists of recognizing the intricate web of connections between yourself and the environment and acknowledging the impact of individual actions on the planet. It involves embracing sustainable practices, advocating for conservation efforts, and nurturing a respectful and symbiotic relationship with nature. Environmental awareness empowers individuals to become stewards of the planet, fostering a collective commitment to safeguarding the Earth for present and future generations.

True success is not about working yourself to exhaustion or sacrificing your well-being for external achievements. It is about aligning your body, mind, and spirit to operate at your highest potential. Holistic wellness is not separate from success; it is the foundation that allows you to build, grow, and sustain it.

SUCCESS PRINCIPLE

Holistic Well-Being refers to a comprehensive, balanced approach to your health and wellness and includes the following components: *physical health, mental and emotional health, social connections, spiritual wellness, occupational wellness, and environmental awareness.* Having a supportive health routine will enhance your energy levels, improve your mental clarity, and foster emotional resilience. It will also enable you to build and maintain meaningful social connections, find purpose in your spiritual practices, and thrive in your professional endeavors. If success is what you desire, then begin with the success of your well-being and how you nurture each aspect of your life.

SUCCESS MINDSET

As an individual seeking success, learn to integrate the holistic components into your life to attain peak health and happiness. Prioritize each aspect by nurturing physical, mental, emotional, and social well-being for balance and fulfillment. Aim to advocate for work-life harmony, recognizing its pivotal role in overall well-being. Continuously seek resources and support systems and destigmatize mental health to foster a culture of encouragement and assistance.

Aligning your health with holistic well-being builds a foundation for a balanced and fulfilling life. Physical health ensures you have the energy to pursue your dreams, while mental and emotional well-being anchor your mind and helps you manage stress and maintain a positive mindset. Building strong social connections enriches your life with support and belonging, while spiritual wellness guides you toward a deeper understanding of your values and purpose. Occupational wellness allows you to find joy and fulfillment in your work, and environmental awareness connects you to the world around you, promoting sustainability and respect for our planet. By integrating these principles into your daily routine, you not only enhance your immediate quality of life, but also set yourself on a path to long-term success and happiness. Start prioritizing your holistic well-being today and unlock your full potential for a thriving, balanced, and purposeful life.

Suggested ways to implement holistic health in various aspects of your life:

1. **Physical Health**
   - **Exercise Regularly:** Incorporate a mix of cardiovascular, strength training, and flexibility exercises into your routine. Aim for at least thirty minutes of moderate exercise most days of the week.
   - **Balanced Nutrition:** Focus on a diet rich in whole foods, including fruits, vegetables, lean proteins, and whole grains. Avoid processed foods and excessive sugar.
   - **Adequate Sleep:** Prioritize getting seven to nine hours of quality sleep each night. Create a relaxing bedtime routine and maintain a consistent sleep schedule.
   - **Hydration:** Drink plenty of water throughout the day. Aim for at least eight glasses to keep your body hydrated and functioning optimally.

2. **Mental and Emotional Well-being**
   - **Mindfulness Meditation:** Practice mindfulness or meditation daily to reduce stress, enhance focus, and promote emotional stability.
   - **Journaling:** Keep a journal to process emotions, reflect on your experiences, and set goals. This can help you gain clarity and reduce anxiety.

- **Daily Gratitude:** Incorporate a gratitude practice into your routine. Each day, write down three things you are grateful for to foster a positive mindset.
- **Set Boundaries:** Learn to say no and set boundaries to protect your mental and emotional health. Prioritize self-care and personal time.

3. Social Connections

- **Foster Relationships:** Make an effort to build and maintain meaningful connections with family, friends, and colleagues. Schedule regular catch-ups and be present in your interactions.
- **Community Involvement:** Engage in community activities or join groups that align with your interests. This can help you build a sense of belonging and a support network.
- **Effective Communication:** Practice active listening and open communication to strengthen your relationships. Be empathetic and understanding toward others.

4. Spiritual Wellness

- **Self-Reflection:** Dedicate time for self-reflection and introspection. Explore your values and beliefs and what brings you purpose and fulfillment.
- **Spiritual Practices:** Engage in spiritual practices that resonate with you, such as meditation, prayer, or spending time in nature.

- **Purpose-Driven Activities:** Match your actions with your core values and pursue activities that give you a sense of purpose and meaning.

5. Occupational Wellness

- **Career Alignment:** Choose a career that aligns with your values and interests. Seek roles that provide satisfaction and fulfillment.
- **Work-Life Balance:** Strive for a healthy work-life balance by setting work and personal time boundaries. Take regular **breaks and avoid overworking.**
- **Professional Development:** Invest in continuous learning and skill development to stay engaged and motivated in your career.

6. Environmental Awareness

- **Sustainable Practices:** Adopt eco-friendly habits such as recycling, reducing waste, and conserving energy. Choose sustainable products and reduce your carbon footprint.
- **Nature Connection:** Spend time outdoors and connect with nature. This can enhance your well-being and foster a sense of environmental stewardship.
- **Advocate for Conservation:** Support and participate in conservation efforts. Educate yourself and others about environmental issues and their impact.

By integrating these holistic health practices into your life, health practices into your life, you can achieve a greater sense of balance and well-being that supports success. As you develop strategies to support this lifestyle, you will experience increased vitality, mental clarity, and emotional resilience, enabling you to handle life's challenges gracefully and confidently. Embracing a holistic approach fosters a deeper connection with yourself and the world around you.

SUCCESS CODE: **HOLISTIC WELL-BEING**

Balance your mind, body, emotions, and energy for lasting success.

CHAPTER 6

THE RESILIENCE CODE

The Ability To Bounce Back From Challenges
Is The Key To Long-Term Success.

In a world that often feels like a whirlwind of opportunities and obstacles, having resilience becomes your greatest ally. As millennials, you are navigating an era blossoming with possibility, yet intertwined with systemic challenges that test your patience, passion, and perseverance. But here's the thing about resilience; it is not just about bouncing back from setbacks, it is about using them as stepping stones to rise higher than ever before.

I know this because my journey is shaped by the relentless pursuit of hope and equity. Growing up in a world marred by segregation, I witnessed the devastating impact of exclusion firsthand. Imagine standing outside a door labeled as 'off-limits' simply because of the color of your skin, the deep sting of inequality piercing through every fiber of your being. These moments were my crucible, where I learned that life's harshest realities could forge a spirit of unstoppable determination. I discovered that adversity, not comfort, shapes and strengthens resilience.

You, too, have the power to take life's trials and turn them into triumphs. Whether you are fighting for inclusion in your workplace, advocating for social justice, or simply striving to be understood, resilience is your anchor. It is the mindset that enables you to rise above challenges, embrace your unique perspective, and see setbacks not as barriers but as springboards for growth.

Succeeding in anything is about mastering resilience. It is about understanding that the power to overcome lies not in avoiding life's storms but in learning to maneuver with them. By harnessing the strength within you and leaning into your experiences, you can transform challenges into opportunities to create a world that values you, celebrates your efforts, and thrives on the strength and determination you exude. Resilience is your compass. It will guide you to embrace the unknown, adapt to change, and emerge as a force for transformation in both your life and the lives of others.

Growing up in South Africa during the era of segregation was not just challenging for me; it was a test of the human spirit within me. I vividly remember that moment when I was denied access to a public restroom simply because of my race. It was not just a physical barrier; it was a deeply emotional and dehumanizing experience. Standing there, I felt a flood of emotions: anger at the injustice, sadness over the exclusion, and a quiet resolve that this was not the world I wanted to accept. Back then, speaking up would get me into trouble with the law, and I would be beaten by the police.

That moment planted a seed of resilience within me. It pushed me to look beyond my immediate struggles and focus on the bigger picture of building a life where such barriers would not hold me back. In that moment of rejection and inequality, I began to understand that adversity, no matter how harsh, carries within it the power to transform. It taught me to rise above, channel the pain into purpose, and use my voice to challenge the very systems that created such injustices.

Looking back, I realize that experience was not merely a challenge to endure. It was a pivotal moment that defined my character. It reinforced my belief in the power of resilience, not just as a means of surviving adversity, but as a tool to create meaningful change. I used the pain of that moment and transformed what it represented into a source of strength and determination, driving me to create environments where diversity, equality, and inclusion are not just ideals but lived realities. I had to use the power of resilience to overcome the conditioning and foster change. It would have been easy to let that situation limit my life. Instead, I used my resilience to ensure that it became the reason behind what I do to make a difference globally.

In today's rapidly changing world, resilience plays a pivotal role in how you experience your personal and professional life. Whether adapting to the gig economy, embracing lifelong learning to stay relevant in evolving industries, or championing diversity and inclusion in multicultural teams, resilience empowers you to overcome setbacks and foster growth.

Resilience also helps you to advocate for those things most important to you. It supports emotional balance and strengthens relationships. As mental health awareness grows, resilience prioritizes wellness for yourself and others, breaking stigmas and promoting safe spaces for everyone. Integrating resilience into your actions and attitudes can drive meaningful change in your communities and families. Imagine the impact you can make going forward versus giving in or giving up. The *Resilience Code* ensures that whatever challenges life delivers your way, you see them as the stepping stones toward a better and more fulfilling experience.

SUCCESS PRINCIPLE

Resilience is the foundation of transformation. It is the inner strength that allows you to face adversity head-on, adapt to changing circumstances, and emerge with a renewed determination. Resilience teaches you that setbacks are not the end of the road but stepping stones to growth and self-discovery. When life presents challenges, resilience empowers you to pause, reflect, and draw upon your inner resources to find a way forward. It transforms obstacles into opportunities for learning, ensuring that, even in the face of difficulty, you continue to progress toward your goals.

Building resilience also equips you to make a greater impact on the world. By learning the ability to rise above challenges, you inspire others to do the same, sparking a chain reaction of strength and empowerment. Resilience also fosters the confidence to advocate for self and others, even when faced with opposition. It must remind you that meaningful change is rarely easy, but always worth pursuing. We can be the catalyst for so many positive things if we are willing to be committed and resilient.

SUCCESS MINDSET

Adopting a mindset of resilience means viewing challenges as opportunities for transformation rather than roadblocks. It requires embracing the belief that every difficulty carries a lesson, every failure contributes to growth, and every setback can lead to a stronger version of yourself. This reflective mindset urges you to shift your perspective from asking, *"Why is this happening to me?"* to *"What can I learn from this?"* With this outlook, you not only endure adversity but emerge from it with greater strength, clarity, and purpose.

To cultivate a resilient mindset, create your personal 'Resilience Roadmap' by defining what is most important to you and how you can stay consistently resilient.

1. **Identify Key Challenges that have occurred in your life. For example:**

   Challenge 1 - Losing a job unexpectedly.

   · Emotional Response: initial shock, fear of financial instability, and feelings of inadequacy.

   Challenge 2 - Navigating a toxic work environment.

   · Emotional Response: stress, frustration, and a decline in self-confidence.

Challenge 3 - Facing rejection after applying to graduate school.

- Emotional Response: disappointment and questioning of my academic and professional goals.

2. **Reflect on the growth that has transpired due to that situation. For example:**

Challenge 1 - You learned to trust in your adaptability and resourcefulness.

- You realized the importance of having a financial safety net and maintaining a growth-oriented mindset.

Challenge 2 - Building emotional resilience and the courage to prioritize your mental well-being over external pressures.

- That experience helped you understand your values and seek environments aligned with your principles.

Challenge 3 - Helped strengthen your perseverance and commitment to long-term goals.

- The rejection pushed you to improve and ultimately made the acceptance even more rewarding.

3. **Extract some key lessons that may be repeating themselves or have shown up to foster new growth in you and create a new action step. For example:**

   Challenge 1 - Willing to shift to a new opportunity
   - Actions to take: update my resume, reach out to my network, and research opportunities to improve my skills.

   Challenge 2 - Becoming a leader in creating a great work environment
   - Actions to take: start practicing mindfulness, create instances of unity and camaraderie, and foster advice from mentors.

   Challenge 3 - Bettering oneself and increasing opportunities
   - Actions to take: analyze feedback, work on strengthening weaker areas, and increasing skills while making a revised plan.

4. **Create connections, lean on a support system, and find others with a similar mindset.**
   - Resilience is not about avoiding failure, but learning to rise stronger every time. Building a support system and taking actionable steps during challenges are crucial to navigating life's uncertainties.
   - Identify three people in your support system whom you can rely on during challenging times. Reach out to one of them and share a current challenge you're facing. Ask for their perspective and support.

- If you're feeling isolated, consider joining online groups, networking events, or finding a mentor who can offer guidance and feedback when you're struggling.

Our resilience is enhanced when we see the ways in which all situations support us in our personal growth and self-development. By having a *Resilience Roadmap* to review situations and identify the benefits and bonuses from them, we align ourselves with true success. Use this exercise to build connections with others who can provide emotional support, encouragement, and perspective. Forming strong relationships with friends, family, mentors, and colleagues will help you navigate difficult times more effectively and remind you of the resilience you inherently possess.

SUCCESS CODE: **RESILIENCE UNLEASHED**

Resilience is forged in adversity, not comfort. Embrace challenges as stepping stones to growth.

YOUR INNER SUCCESS EQUALS YOUR OUTER SUCCESS

Redefining 'Being Holistic' Using Emotional Intelligence, Resilience, Mission, Drive, And Purpose-Minded Codes.

A s you finish this first part of the inner *Success Codes,* I hope you're beginning to see just how powerful you truly are. You've learned how to redefine success, nurture your well-being, build resilience, and align your goals with your purpose. Each one of these has laid the foundation for something extraordinary. These codes are all about self-reflection and personal growth within your success mindset. They show how to create a life that feels meaningful and authentic to you, a life where your values guide your path and your inner strength shines through in everything you do.

I know this journey inward can sometimes feel challenging, but it's also where the most profound transformations happen. Every step you've taken has brought you closer to understanding who you are at your core. That self-awareness and clarity are the greatest tools you have in building the life you want. It's not just about reaching milestones or ticking boxes. It's about becoming the person who wakes up each day with purpose, confidence, and a deep sense of fulfillment.

Now, as we prepare to move forward, you might be wondering, *How do I take all this personal growth and bring it into the world around me? How do I turn this foundation into action, into tangible results in my career, my relationships, and my goals?*

That's exactly where we're headed next.

In the next section, we will focus on applying everything you've learned about yourself to the external world. This is where you will discover how to create success in your professional life, build strong and meaningful connections, and navigate the opportunities and challenges that come your way with grace and confidence. The internal work you've done is not separate from your external achievements. They go hand in hand. When you align with your values and purpose, success in the world becomes not only possible but inevitable.

I believe in your potential. Millennials are often described as a generation of seekers desiring purpose, balance, and deeper connection. But what I see is a generation of leaders, innovators, and changemakers. You are not just here to follow a path. You are here to create one. You are here to redefine what success looks like, not just for yourself but for your communities and the generations that will follow.

As we move forward, stay open to the opportunities that lie ahead. The work you have done within yourself is the key to unlocking success in every part of your life. The next step is about bringing that foundation into the world and watching it grow.

BUILDING YOUR PERSONAL SUCCESS

Deepen Your Awareness, Connect With Your Core, And Honor Your Internal Foundation.

Before anything great can be built, the foundation must be strong. This part of the journey was about reconnecting with your truth—your values, your health, your purpose. Now, it's time to pause and reflect. Not just to think but to feel. To ask, *where have I been hiding from myself? Where have I been strong? What truths have I remembered that I want to carry with me?*

You are the most important project you will ever work on. So, let's check in with you.

Reflection Prompts:

· In what ways has my definition of success evolved in these chapters?

_____

_____

· What habits or beliefs am I ready to release to support my growth?

_____

_____

· How has focusing on my well-being influenced how I see my future?

_____

_____

· Where in my life am I living out of alignment with who I truly am?

_____

_____

· What values or inner strengths am I proud to embody right now?

_____

_____

Action Steps:

· Write down three self-care practices that nourish you. Commit to one this week.

_____

_____

· Identify one way you can be more compassionate with yourself each day.

_____

_____

Choose a word that reflects how you want to feel. Begin your morning with that word as a guide.

_____

_____

Reflect on a moment of personal resilience. What did it teach you?

_____

_____

TWO

External Application

SUCCEEDING IN THE WORLD

Our Inner Understanding Of Success Is Reflected In The
Impact We Make Externally.

O nce you've built a strong internal foundation, the next step is
applying those principles to the world around you. Personal
success is only the beginning. True fulfillment comes when you can
take what you've learned about yourself and use it to create opportunities, build relationships, and navigate the complexities of your
career, finances, and broader life goals.

As the world evolves and demand increases, success will no longer
be just about having the right skills or knowledge. It will be about
adaptability, innovation, and connectedness. The most successful
people aren't just those who work hard, they are the ones who embrace
change, build strong networks, and create environments that support
their personal growth and professional ambitions.

Think of people like Michelle Obama, Richard Branson, and Steve Jobs. Their success wasn't just a result of internal clarity. They knew how to take their values and vision and apply them in the real world.

Michelle Obama didn't just succeed because of her education or background. She built her influence through authentic leadership, a focus on community, and the ability to connect with people from all walks of life. Her success reflects how she applies her personal values of service, resilience, and empowerment to make a tangible impact on society.

Richard Branson is known for his adventurous spirit and bold business ventures. But his success goes beyond risk-taking. He created a company culture that values flexibility, creativity, and work-life balance, proving that you can build a thriving business while staying true to your core values.

Steve Jobs wasn't just a tech visionary. He succeeded because he combined his passion for innovation with a relentless commitment to design, simplicity, and user experience. His ability to adapt and lead with vision transformed not just Apple™ but entire industries.

Now that you've done the internal work, it's your turn to step into the world with the same clarity and purpose. The foundation you've built within yourself isn't meant to stay hidden. It's meant to guide how you show up in your career, your relationships, and your goals. You have everything you need to take your personal growth and turn it into tangible success, not just for yourself but for the people and communities you'll impact along the way.

In this section, we'll dive into the codes that will help you succeed in the world. You'll learn how to stay adaptable in a rapidly evolving environment, build financial stability, create fulfilling work cultures, and foster meaningful connections. These are the practical applications of the internal work you've done, giving you the tools to thrive in both your personal and professional life.

As you read through these chapters, consider how you can integrate these codes into your daily actions. *How can you align your career with your values? By building relationships, how can you better support your growth? How can you stay flexible in the face of change while staying true to your purpose?*

This is where it all comes together. The goals you've been dreaming about, the life you've envisioned, they're within reach when you apply the lessons you've learned. You're no longer just reacting to life's challenges; you're creating a path forward that's aligned with your values and purpose. The difference between where you are now and where you want to be lies in how you take the tools from your internal journey and use them to build a life that's not only successful but deeply meaningful.

Success isn't just about what you know, it's about how you apply it. And when you bring your internal foundation into alignment with your external actions, you create a life that is not only successful but sustainable and deeply rewarding.

CHAPTER 7

THE COMMUNITY & NETWORKING CODE

Success Thrives In Connection. Your Relationships
Are Your Greatest Asset.

Success is not just about individual effort. It is deeply influenced by the strength and alignment of the networks we build. Reflecting on my journey from working in a factory to leading impactful initiatives, I recognize how pivotal connections have been in shaping my growth. Each relationship introduced me to new perspectives, ideas, and challenges that pushed me beyond what I thought was possible. The right connections opened doors, provided mentorship, and helped me develop the confidence to pursue bigger opportunities. Without the support and guidance of key people along the way, my path would have been much harder to navigate.

For your generation, networking is more than just a way to climb the career ladder. It is an opportunity to build a community that fuels both personal and professional growth. Success is rarely a solo journey.

The power of networking is not just in expanding your circle, rather in creating spaces where people from all backgrounds can collaborate, share knowledge, and thrive together. A more diverse network exposes you to new ways of thinking and innovative ideas. Strong networks create access to new opportunities, inspire fresh perspectives, and provide support through every stage of growth.

Networking is not just about what you can gain. It is equally about what you can contribute. Building meaningful relationships requires more than just making connections. It is about being intentional in how you engage, bringing value to others, and fostering relationships based on trust and mutual support. The most successful people do not just collect contacts; they cultivate relationships by offering help, sharing resources, and supporting others in their goals. Whether through mentorship, collaboration, or simply showing up for others, the connections you build today will shape the opportunities you create for the future.

Technology has made networking easier than ever, but it has also made it more important to be authentic. Social media and digital platforms allow you to connect with people across the world, but genuine connections are built through meaningful conversations and authentic engagement. It is not about how many followers you have or how many LinkedIn™ requests you send. It is about the quality of your interactions and the depth of the relationships you cultivate.

True networking is about alignment. It is about surrounding yourself with people who challenge you, inspire you, and encourage you to grow. Your network should reflect your values, your ambitions, and your commitment to continuous learning. Seek those who share your vision and those who bring different perspectives and challenge you to think bigger. When you build a strong, purpose-driven network, you do not just create opportunities for yourself. You create a ripple effect that uplifts and empowers others.

One of the most rewarding parts of my journey has been connecting with the *Ignite Humanity*™ community, a global network of change makers united by the shared mission of uplifting others. Through this network, I have collaborated with individuals from diverse walks of life, each bringing unique talents, stories, and perspectives to the table. This connection also allowed me the opportunity to become an international best-selling author twice. Whether brainstorming ideas for community initiatives or supporting one another's endeavors, the collective energy has been transformative. These connections have taught me the value of building bridges across differences, seeing humanity in one another, and understanding that diversity in thought and experience often leads to the most innovative solutions.

Networking in today's landscape is about creating meaningful con-nections that drive collective progress. Communities that thrive do so because they emphasize inclusion, shared goals, and authentic relationships. Whether you are mentoring someone in your field, collaborating across industries, or building niche groups with common interests, the key is to approach every interaction with curiosity and a willingness to add value. When you build bridges with sincerity and purpose, your network becomes your strength, helping you navigate challenges, discover opportunities, and achieve success that's rooted in community.

There is a famous quote by Porter Gale, "Your network is your net worth." This statement holds more truth today than ever before. The relationships you cultivate have the power to shape your opportunities, open doors you never knew existed, and accelerate your personal and professional growth.

Your network is not just a collection of contacts. It is a living, evolving ecosystem of people who influence your mindset, challenge your thinking, and provide access to resources and opportunities. The stronger and more intentional your network is, the more valuable it becomes. It is not about simply knowing people. It is about fostering meaningful relationships that create mutual growth and support.

Think about the most successful people in any industry. They did not reach their positions alone. Behind every great leader, entrepreneur, or changemaker is a network of mentors, collaborators, and supporters who helped them navigate challenges and seize opportunities. Your network can introduce you to new ways of thinking, connect you with the right people, and encourage you to take bold steps forward.

At the same time, networking is not just about personal gain. The most impactful networks are built on a foundation of generosity and reciprocity. When you contribute value to others, whether through sharing knowledge, making introductions, or offering support, you strengthen the bonds within your network. Over time, these relationships create a cycle of opportunities that benefit everyone involved.

Success is rarely achieved in isolation. By investing in meaningful connections, you are not just building a network. You are building a foundation for long-term growth, impact, and success.

SUCCESS PRINCIPLE

Community and Networking is about building bridges and forging unity. The foundation of true success lies in fostering genuine connections within communities and building networks that extend beyond your comfort zones. When you prioritize relationships over transactions, you create bridges that enable shared growth and mutual support. Trust, collaboration, and a shared sense of purpose build strong communities, where every connection offers opportunities to learn, grow, and contribute to a collective vision. By actively engaging with diverse groups and embracing the value of giving before receiving, you can transform your network into a thriving ecosystem of opportunity and support.

A community's power is its ability to bring people together for a common purpose and amplify their potential. Building meaningful networks is more accessible than ever, even for those who find traditional networking events intimidating. For introverts, small-group settings or virtual meetups can provide a comfortable space to connect with like-minded individuals. Online communities and forums can also serve as valuable avenues for building relationships in a focused, low-pressure environment. For instance, a case study of a graphic designer who built a thriving freelance business entirely through participation in an online creative community shows how digital tools can break down barriers. By offering advice, sharing work, and engaging in thoughtful conversations, anyone can create strong, supportive networks without having to compromise their comfort zones.

When it comes to building networks, it's easy to stay within comfortable circles, whether they revolve around a specific industry, culture, or shared interests. However, the most meaningful growth happens when we intentionally step outside these boundaries to connect with people who challenge us to think differently. Imagine the impact of engaging with individuals from diverse backgrounds, industries, and geographies, all bringing fresh insights and opportunities.

Social media has revolutionized the way you can connect and collaborate, offering opportunities beyond traditional professional platforms. It allows for real-time conversations around specific interests while visual storytelling apps authentically showcase your important message. Engaging authentically, commenting thoughtfully, sharing valuable content, and participating in live discussions can help create genuine relationships across various platforms and social tools. A personal trainer grew their business by sharing fitness tips online, responding to followers' questions, and joining fitness-related conversations. This is a prime example of how social platforms can foster connections that are both personal and professional. By approaching social media as a tool for collaboration and learning rather than mere self-promotion, millennials can tap into a vast, diverse network of individuals eager to engage, share, and grow together.

Building a strong network and engaging with a thriving community is not just a strategy for success. It is a mindset that prioritizes connection, collaboration, and shared growth. A willingness to connect builds the most impactful relationships. Whether through in-person interactions, online communities, or meaningful conversations on social media, every connection holds the potential to open doors, spark new ideas, and create a lasting impact.

When you invest in relationships with intention, you are not just building a network; you are cultivating a support system that fuels both your personal and professional growth. True success is not about how many people you know. It is about the depth of the connections you build and the value you bring to those relationships.

SUCCESS MINDSET

True success is not achieved in isolation but through the power of community and meaningful connections. For me, the learning was to cultivate a *collaborative spirit*. Embracing a mindset of collaboration allows you to see networking as a two-way exchange, where giving and receiving support lead to shared growth. A networking and community mindset values genuine relationships, approaches interactions with an open mind, and focuses on collective success rather than individual gain. Anyone can build a network that empowers both you and those around you. Having this mindset transforms networking from a transactional activity into a fulfilling journey of mutual enrichment.

Below are some pointers that you can use to cultivate a thriving network and a sense of belonging that empowers both individual and collective success:

1. Define Your Purpose for Networking

- Reflect on why you want to network. *Are you seeking mentorship, career opportunities, or a community with shared values?*
- Understanding your goals helps you approach networking with clarity and confidence.

2. **Start with Authentic Relationships**
   - Focus on building genuine connections rather than transactional ones.
   - Listen actively, show genuine interest, and seek ways to add value to others' lives.

3. **Leverage Online Communities**
   - Join digital spaces that align with your interests or professional goals.
   - Be active by engaging in discussions, sharing insights, and supporting others.

4. **Create Your Own Tribe**
   - If you can't find a community that fits your needs, build one! Start a book club, hiking group, or an online forum for a shared interest or cause.
   - Encourage inclusivity and participation to foster collaboration.

5. **Balance Giving and Receiving**
   - Approach networking with a mindset of giving before receiving. Share your expertise, offer support, and celebrate others' successes.
   - Be open to asking for help or advice when needed, creating a reciprocal relationship.

6. **Embrace Diversity in Your Network**
   - Step out of your comfort zone and connect with people from different industries, cultures, and perspectives.
   - Attend cross-disciplinary events or collaborate with individuals outside your usual circle to broaden your horizons.

7. **Utilize Social Media Wisely**
   - Use various social media platforms to connect authentically.
   - Share valuable content that reflects your personal brand and engage with posts from others meaningfully.

8. **Stay Consistent and Follow Up**
   - Networking is not a one-time activity, it requires consistency.
   - Follow up with new connections, express gratitude, and nurture relationships over time.

9. **Engage in Small-Group or One-on-One Settings**
   - For introverts, smaller settings can feel less overwhelming. Attend intimate gatherings, take part in workshops, or schedule one-on-one coffee chats.

10. **Track Your Progress and Reflect**
   - Periodically evaluate the growth and quality of your network.
   - Reflect on how your connections have contributed to your personal and professional development and how you've added value to others.

The strength of your community and network is one of the most powerful assets you will ever build. People rarely achieve success alone. It is shaped by the people you surround yourself with, the conversations you engage in, and the relationships you nurture over time. Success is not just about what you achieve individually, it's also about how you contribute to something greater.

When you focus on building strong, meaningful connections, you are not just opening doors for yourself. You are creating a cumulative effect that lifts others and amplifies your impact.

SUCCESS CODE:
CONNECTED GROWTH

Success thrives in community,
networking with purpose,
and growing together.

CHAPTER 8

THE COLLABORATION CODE

Diverse Perspectives And Teamwork Accelerate
Growth And Creativity.

Imagine a workplace where every voice matters. Collaboration is not just a buzzword but a way of life, and the richness of diversity fuels creativity and innovation. As millennials, you are rewriting the playbook for success by championing these principles. You have seen the power of collective effort and understand that the greatest breakthroughs happen when diverse minds come together in harmony. This is not just about meeting goals or hitting targets, it's about building a culture that thrives on empathy, inclusion, and shared purpose. Your approach to collaboration reflects your acceptance of other viewpoints, and welcoming diversity in opinions is reshaping how we define success globally.

Growing up in a world that emphasized connection and collaboration, you likely have already embraced a mindset that values the collective over the individual. Whether in classrooms, startups, or global enterprises, you have seen how pooling diverse perspectives leads to richer solutions. Your generation has a knack for transforming traditional hierarchies into communities of equals, where empathy and shared decision-making pave the way for progress. By focusing on collaboration, you are welcoming new ideas and creating an environment where innovation thrives and everyone feels empowered to contribute.

Collaboration, teamwork, and partnerships are not just ideals. They are transformative forces that define the way you live and work. You have witnessed firsthand how breaking down silos and fostering inclusivity drives meaningful change. By bringing diverse voices into the conversation, you unlock the potential for groundbreaking ideas that reflect the complexity of our interconnected world. It is about more than just unity in numbers, it's about building spaces where people feel they truly belong and allowing them to bring their entire selves to the table.

I am sure we can agree that embracing collaborations is not always easy. Balancing differing perspectives, addressing unconscious biases, and navigating tough conversations require awareness and empathy. Yet, by prioritizing compassion, open dialogue, and continuous understanding, you are bringing people together and shaping a collective that emphasizes the power of unity. You can agree that success is a collective journey fueled by people coming together with common goals and supportive attitudes.

One of the most transformative lessons I have learnt is the immense power of listening and understanding, particularly when championing collaboration. I vividly remember launching programs to raise awareness about mental wellness, a pressing issue among young people. I realized many youths were grappling with their mental health in silence, yearning for supportive environments and accessible resources. By focusing on their stories and needs, I discovered that genuine change starts with bringing people together to foster connectedness and understanding.

Through my efforts, I witnessed the profound impact of collective action. Whether it was working with volunteers, educators, or other advocates, our combined efforts created a ripple effect that empowered countless young people to navigate their challenges and embrace their potential. These experiences deepened my resolve to make collaboration more than a concept, it became a way of life.

Over time, I have extended my collaborative work to include the blind, Deaf, and autistic communities. I carry the belief that when we work together with open hearts and shared goals; we create environments where everyone, regardless of their background or abilities, feels valued and supported. The beauty of coming together lies in accepting our differences and in uniting to create greater change.

In addition to my work with mental wellness and marginalized communities, I have also partnered with cancer associations to raise awareness and support for those affected by this devastating illness. My commitment to collaboration took on a new dimension when I realized the importance of bridging the gap between the Deaf and hearing communities. Through carefully planned initiatives and events, I aimed to create meaningful connections and mutual understanding between these groups. Whether it was arranging interpreters, hosting inclusive workshops, or simply encouraging open communication, these efforts brought people together in ways that transcended barriers. Witnessing the Deaf and hearing communities unite to collaborate on shared causes like cancer awareness reaffirmed my belief that inclusivity is about creating space for everyone and building bridges that strengthen the collective fabric of our society. These experiences continue to fuel my passion.

In our rapidly evolving world, embracing collaboration has become a cornerstone of successful ventures. One shining example is the global company Microsoft™, which has consistently prioritized accessibility and inclusivity in its products and workplace culture. By hiring diverse talent and ensuring a welcoming environment for people with disabilities, the company has improved innovation and created solutions like the Xbox™ Adaptive Controller, which makes gaming accessible to those with limited mobility.

Whitney Wolfe Herd, the founder of Bumble™, transformed the dating industry by emphasizing women's empowerment. Tired of regular dating sites, she 'changed the game' by making Bumble, the only dating site where women make the first move. Today Bumble has 55 million users in 150 countries. Every generation can learn from these success stories to see how prioritizing co-collaboration and shared outcomes can yield tangible, impactful results both in business and in society.

You can apply this success code by fostering collaboration within your own spheres, whether through volunteer efforts, workplace initiatives, or entrepreneurial ventures. For example, tech start-ups like Slack™ have shown how promoting diverse hiring practices and creating safe spaces for employees to share their unique perspectives enhances teamwork and problem-solving. Valuing equity and collaboration can lead the way by embracing these strategies in your own careers. Whether it's mentoring underrepresented groups or using their platforms to advocate for richer collaborations, these actions will ensure they remain active contributors to a more inclusive, innovative, and harmonious society.

SUCCESS PRINCIPLE

Collaboration - This success principle embodies a transformative approach to leadership and achievement for millennials. This principle highlights the power of leaders creating environments that welcome and celebrate diverse perspectives as vital to innovation and progress. You know that collective intelligence thrives when varied voices come together, challenging traditional hierarchies and promoting shared goals. This approach fosters team dynamics rooted in mutual respect, creativity, and equity to demonstrate a commitment to building supportive communities that value every individual's contributions. By embracing this principle, you are reshaping what success looks like, moving away from individualistic gains and toward collective empowerment.

Fully integrating this principle requires an ongoing dedication to personal and collective growth. It involves fostering open communication, actively listening to different viewpoints, and breaking down barriers that impede inclusivity. By prioritizing these actions, you can create cohesive teams and communities where everyone feels valued and empowered to contribute their best. Addressing segregation and promoting unity not only strengthens connections but also leads to innovative and impactful outcomes. This principle underscores that true leadership lies in leveraging the *strength of collaboration* to drive meaningful, lasting success for individuals, organizations, and society as a whole.

SUCCESS MINDSET

Adopting a success mindset focused on collaboration means recognizing the power of collective effort and diverse perspectives in driving growth and innovation. For millennials, the key to success lies in not only embracing diversity but actively fostering environments where inclusivity thrives. By taking intentional steps to promote inclusivity and managing diverse teams effectively, you can create workplaces and communities where every voice is valued and everyone can contribute to the collective success.

Here are five steps you can take to align with the *Collaboration* mindset:

1. **Promote Active Inclusivity**
    *   Move beyond simply encouraging collaboration. Actively promote inclusivity by creating an environment that welcomes everyone's ideas. This could involve setting up mentoring programs that pair individuals from different backgrounds, offering unconscious bias training, or creating spaces where people can share their experiences and learn from one another.

2. **Build a Culture of Belonging**

    · Cultivate a sense of belonging within your team or community by ensuring that every individual feels seen, heard, and valued. Recognize the unique contributions of each person and celebrate diverse perspectives. Create open channels of communication and support initiatives that encourage cross-cultural interactions and shared experiences to achieve this.

3. **Lead with Empathy**

    · As you manage diverse teams, take the time to understand the individual needs, strengths, and challenges of each team member. Approach leadership with empathy, making an effort to listen and understand different viewpoints. Empathy builds trust, which is essential for resolving conflicts and maintaining a collaborative atmosphere.

4. **Resolve Conflicts with Sensitivity**

    · Differences in culture, background, or generational viewpoints can lead to misunderstandings or conflicts within diverse teams. Address these conflicts with sensitivity by encouraging open dialogue and understanding. Create a safe space where differences are respected and resolved through healthy discussions rather than division.

5. Champion Allyship

- Take actionable steps to be an ally for underrepresented individuals within your workplace or community. Support initiatives that promote inclusivity and offer your help to those who may face isolated or judged. Friendship is essential in creating an environment where everyone feels empowered, included, and supported.

Collaboration means letting go of competition and opening your heart and mind to welcome others in. Imagine the impact you can make, success you can achieve, and the connections you can solidify when you widen your perspective and see things from the viewpoint of more people, voices, and perspectives; this equals more success for everyone.

SUCCESS CODE:
COLLABORATIVE INNOVATION

Millennial success thrives on collaborative leadership, empathy, and inclusivity— reshaping workplaces to champion diverse perspectives and value every voice.

CHAPTER 9

THE WORK CULTURE & FLEXIBILITY CODE

Balance And Adaptability Are The New Benchmarks

For A Fulfilling Career.

Workplaces today are evolving in extraordinary ways, thanks largely to the innovative spirit and values of your generation. Many millennials have sparked a movement toward more creative, inclusive, and collaborative work environments, where flexibility is not just a perk but a cornerstone of success. This is not about convenience, it's about creating space for personal growth, self-care, and meaningful contributions while thriving professionally. Work culture and flexibility are essential ingredients for fulfillment, productivity, and purpose.

Looking back on my thirty years in various workplaces, one constant theme stands out; flexibility was never on the table. Work hours were rigid, expectations were unwavering, and the concept of mental well-being was not even part of the conversation. I vividly recall times when important family milestones were missed, hobbies and exercise took a backseat, and the weight of work demands felt suffocating. The lack of adaptability was not just inconvenient, it was deeply draining. The lack of flexibility left little room for self-care, personal growth, or even a sense of balance.

The effects of an inflexible work environment took a toll on my mental well-being. Stress and burnout became familiar companions, and I often felt like I was running on empty. But through those challenges, I learned invaluable lessons about resilience and grit. Every late night, every moment of frustration, taught me how to persevere and push through adversity. These experiences shaped my perspective on the importance of flexible work culture. Now, I understand how vital it is to create environments where people can thrive without sacrificing their personal lives. If I had the chance to work in the flexible environments available today, I imagine I could have achieved growth and fulfillment even earlier in my life. Yet, those struggles shaped me, and today I am here to tell you that when you prioritize work cultures that value balance and adaptability, you are not just improving your job but transforming your future.

Those years of rigidity also gave me a deep appreciation for the changes we are seeing today. The rise of flexible work arrangements, remote options, hybrid models, and adaptable schedules offers something I could only dream of back then; the ability to integrate work with life seamlessly. Today's modern solutions not only foster productivity but also create space for personal growth, self-care, and meaningful connections. Imagine attending your child's school play during the day and still meeting your deadlines in the evening or having the freedom to travel while staying professionally engaged. These possibilities represent a seismic shift in how we define success, no longer tethered to traditional notions of productivity but anchored in holistic well-being.

By reflection on the past and the more traditional workplace structure, I hope to highlight the importance of seeking work environments that prioritize flexibility. My experience showed me that while grit helps you survive hard times, flexibility and good systems help you thrive. Advocate for workplace cultures that allow you to excel both personally and professionally. And remember, success is not just about what you achieve, it's also about how you feel while achieving it.

Modern workplaces are evolving, and many companies are leading the change by embracing flexibility as a cornerstone of their culture. Companies like Google™ and Atlassian™ offer hybrid work models, unlimited PTO, and wellness programs to support employees' work-life balance. Smaller startups, such as Buffer™, have gone fully remote, providing employees with the freedom to work from anywhere while fostering collaboration through innovative communication tools. These organizations demonstrate that flexibility is not just about convenience, it's a strategy for enhancing productivity, creativity, and employee satisfaction. Your generation can take inspiration from these examples when seeking employers or advocating for similar policies in your own workplaces. By prioritizing environments that value inclusivity, adaptability, and mental well-being, you can align your careers with your aspirations and lifestyle.

For those negotiating rigid workplaces, adaptability and proactive communication are key. Start by having an open conversation with your employer about your needs, presenting a clear case for how flexibility could benefit both you and the organization. For example, suggest a trial period for remote work or adjusted hours and emphasize how it could improve productivity and reduce burnout. If changes are not immediately possible, focus on what you can control, establish boundaries around your work hours, prioritize self-care, and find ways to recharge outside of work. Build a support system by connecting with like-minded colleagues or professional networks to share strategies and encouragement. Even in a traditional workplace, small steps toward balance and well-being can create meaningful change and help you thrive.

SUCCESS PRINCIPLE

Work Culture and Flexibility - This approach centers on fostering environments that spark creativity, encourage collaboration, and champion work-life balance. For millennials, success often hinges on workplaces that offer flexible arrangements like remote work options, adaptable schedules, and a focus on well-being. These setups are more than just conveniences, they enable you to balance personal growth with professional excellence. When immersed in a positive and vibrant work culture, you feel engaged, motivated, and less prone to stress or burnout, ultimately leading to greater job satisfaction and overall happiness.

To achieve the ideal work culture and flexibility, look for workplaces that cultivate positivity, are adaptive, and promote flexibility. Seek out companies that offer creative work arrangements, including remote work options and adaptable schedules. Prioritize employers who value open dialogue, mutual respect, and a deep sense of belonging. Advocate for a culture of collaboration and creativity, where your ideas and contributions are encouraged and recognized. Additionally, focus on personal development opportunities within your workplace, such as training programs and mentorship. By choosing environments that align with these values, you will find places where you can truly flourish, both personally and professionally.

Here are some ideas on what to look for when wanting flexibility and a positive culture in the workplace.

1. **Identify Your Work Values and Goals**
   - Reflect on what matters most to you in a work environment. This could include aspects like flexibility, inclusivity, creativity, or collaboration. Once you've identified these values, set clear goals for what you want to achieve, both professionally and personally. This clarity will help you choose or negotiate for a work environment that supports these goals.

2. **Seek Flexible Work Arrangements**
   - Explore remote work options or discuss alternate possibilities with your employer. Highlight the benefits, such as increased productivity and reduced commuting stress. Consider negotiating flexible work hours that fit your lifestyle and suggest trial periods to demonstrate how flexibility can enhance your performance.

3. **Create a Positive Work Environment**
   - Engage with team members in collaborative projects that leverage each person's strengths, fostering a sense of belonging and teamwork.

4. Enhance Work-Life Balance

- Incorporate self-care activities into your daily routine, such as exercise, meditation, or hobbies, to recharge and maintain balance. Practice time management techniques to stay focused during work hours, allowing you to maximize productivity and free up personal time.

5. Continuously Assess and Adjust

- Periodically assess your work environment and its alignment with your values and goals. Make adjustments as needed to stay on track. Solicit feedback from peers and supervisors to gain insights into your performance and areas for improvement, and use this information to enhance your work experience.

SUCCESS MINDSET

Embrace the idea that a thriving work environment is not just a luxury but a necessity for your well-being and professional growth. Understand that flexible work arrangements, such as remote work and adaptable schedules, are crucial for maintaining a healthy work-life balance. Approach your career with the belief that you deserve to work in a place that values creativity, collaboration, and inclusivity.

Seek out workplaces that foster open dialogue, mutual respect, and a sense of belonging. By adopting this mindset, you will not only enhance your productivity and job satisfaction, but also ensure that your work reflects your personal values and life goals. Remember, a flexible and supportive work culture empowers you to bring your best self to work every day, paving the way for long-term success and fulfillment.

Here are five steps to help you align with this mindset and thrive:

1. **Define Your Ideal Work Environment**
   - Reflect on what work culture and flexibility mean to you. Identify the elements that are inline with your values and long-term goals. Seek workplaces that prioritize these aspects, or create a vision of how you can incorporate flexibility into your existing environment.

2. Pursue Opportunities for Growth and Balance

- Strive for roles that offer both professional development and room for personal well-being. Show how work-life balance can benefit both you and the organization, emphasizing increased productivity and morale.

3. Invest in Skills that Enhance Adaptability

- Flexibility often comes from being prepared to adapt to new challenges and opportunities. By enhancing your expertise, you open doors to flexible roles that suit your lifestyle and goals.

4. Prioritize Your Well-Being

- Balance is essential for maintaining a positive mindset. Schedule time for self-care, hobbies, and relationships to prevent burnout and maintain focus. A balanced approach will empower you to perform at your best, both professionally and personally.

By implementing these practical actions, you can create a work environment that supports your well-being and professional growth, and also resonates with your personal values and life goals. Embracing a flexible and supportive work culture empowers you to bring your best self to work every day, paving the way for long-term success and fulfillment.

Additionally, the most important part is to recognize that your mental well-being is paramount. A supportive work culture that prioritizes flexibility allows you to manage stress more effectively and maintain a healthy work-life integration. It gives you the freedom to pursue personal interests and passions *outside* of work, leading to a more balanced and fulfilling life overall. When you feel valued and supported in your workplace, you're more likely to contribute positively, work better in a team, and achieve meaningful career milestones. I encourage you to embrace this mindset of balance and flexibility and seek opportunities that align with your vision for a fulfilling and successful career journey.

SUCCESS CODE: **FLEXIBLE SUCCESS**

Thrive in flexible, inclusive work cultures for personal and professional growth.

CHAPTER 10

THE CONTINUOUS LEARNING CODE

Real Success Unfolds When You Begin To Master Your
Craft By Being A Talented Student.

Continuous learning and growth for millennials is about embracing a mindset that values ongoing education and self-improvement. It means recognizing that success is not a static destination but a journey that requires constant adaptation and enhancement of skills. You must proactively pursue new knowledge and experiences to enrich both your personal and professional life. It's about being curious, open-minded, and willing to step out of your comfort zone to gain new competencies and perspectives. In a rapidly changing professional landscape, continuous learning and growth are essential for staying relevant and competitive.

A top *Success Code* is continuously learning and growing. Prioritizing a commitment to constant self-improvement will distinguish you from others in the field. Embracing personal and professional development opportunities, whether through formal education, workshops, mentorship, or self-directed learning, will have you standing out amongst the crowd. By constantly evolving and expanding your capabilities, you'll stay ahead of the curve and position yourself for long-term success in the ever-changing entrepreneurial landscape.

Having a keen desire to learn can profoundly impact you by empowering yourself to navigate and thrive in an ever-evolving job market. This approach fosters resilience and adaptability, critical traits in an era of technological advancements and constant change. By committing to lifelong learning, you can better position yourself for career advancement and long-term fulfillment. It also enhances your problem-solving abilities, creativity, and innovation, making you a valuable asset in any organization. This dedication to self-improvement often results in more job satisfaction and a stronger sense of purpose, aligning with intrinsic motivation to achieve and excel.

My first job as a sweeper and packer in a factory required no continuous learning from me. Yet, during one of my twelve-hour night shifts, a voice asked me, *Is this where you want to be for the rest of your life, Nolan?*

It was so real, like this voice was reading my mind and shouting down at me. I do not know if it was God or my Higher Purpose, but the question was valid. My immediate answer was, "No." I instantly paused, fluctuating between thoughts of inspiration like *I CAN do more* and self-doubt such, as *I am just a packer/sweeper and do not have my grade twelve metric.* Fear bounced around in my head and threatened to keep me standing still as I wondered whether I had what it took to pursue an actual career. Except the voice repeatedly asked, *Do you want to be here?* I could not deny the answer in my heart. *No.* As I embraced the truth, new courage grew within me, and I knew I must focus on continuous learning to improve my life. This eventually led to massive growth opportunities both in my personal and professional life.

I encourage you to reflect on the moments when you felt most challenged. *Were there times when you stepped into the unknown, learned something new, or overcame a difficult obstacle?* These experiences often create a sense of urgency and purpose, reminding us that growth happens when we push our boundaries and desire to learn more. By continuously seeking new learning opportunities, you open yourself up to endless possibilities and pave the way for both personal and professional breakthroughs. Often, we must embrace the discomfort that comes with growth, knowing that each step forward enhances our capabilities for more.

Think about the areas in your life where you have untapped potential. Perhaps there are skills you've always wanted to develop or subjects you're passionate about but never had the chance to explore.

Now is the time to invest in yourself. Set aside dedicated time for personal development, whether it's reading a book, taking an online course, or engaging in meaningful conversations with mentors and peers. By nurturing a growth mindset and committing to lifelong learning, you empower yourself to navigate the complexities of life with confidence and creativity. Remember, every small step you take toward self-improvement brings you closer to realizing your fullest potential.

SUCCESS PRINCIPLE

Continuous Learning and Growth - For everyone, continuous learning and personal growth are essential to achieving lasting success. One must understand that success is an ongoing journey, not a destination, demanding a consistent pursuit of knowledge and skill enhancement. You can stay relevant and competitive in a rapidly changing world by fostering curiosity and proactivity. Having this mindset develops your capabilities and adaptability, which are crucial for navigating the ever-evolving job market. A dedication to lifelong learning will improve career opportunities and personal satisfaction, thereby increasing the capacity for problem-solving, creativity, and innovation. The following action items will guide your ability to stay ahead in a rapidly evolving world.

To make it both easy and fun, here are some suggestions for you to implement:

- **Make** it a priority to constantly seek new knowledge and skills that syncs with your passions and career goals. Doing so enhances your expertise and ensures that your professional development is meaningful and fulfilling. This proactive approach allows you to stay ahead of industry trends and technological advancements, making you a valuable asset in your field.

- **Engage** in formal education, attend workshops, and pursue mentorship opportunities to gain valuable insights and practical advice. Formal education provides a solid foundation and in-depth understanding of your chosen field, equipping you with the theoretical knowledge necessary to excel. Workshops offer hands-on experience and exposure to the latest tools, techniques, and best practices, allowing you to apply what you've learned in real-world scenarios. Pursuing mentorship opportunities connects you with experienced professionals who can offer personalized guidance, share their expertise, and help you navigate your career path.

- **Utilize** online resources, books, and podcasts to explore diverse subjects at your own pace. These tools offer flexible and accessible ways to expand your knowledge and skills, allowing you to learn whenever and wherever it suits you. Online resources, such as educational platforms and webinars, provide up-to-date information and interactive learning experiences. Books offer in-depth exploration of topics, enabling you to dive deeply into areas of interest. Podcasts bring expert insights and diverse perspectives directly to you.

- **Adopt** a growth mindset, viewing challenges as opportunities for development. Believe that you can develop your abilities and intelligence through dedication and hard work. When faced with obstacles, see them as chances to learn and grow rather than setbacks.

- **Prioritize** self-reflection and mindfulness practices to better understand your strengths and areas for improvement. Regular self-reflection helps you to evaluate your experiences, recognize your accomplishments, and identify areas where you can grow. Mindfulness practices, such as meditation and journaling, enable you to stay present and attuned to your thoughts and emotions, fostering greater self-awareness.

- **Embrace** lifelong learning by watching educational videos that inspire and challenge your thinking. These videos offer dynamic and engaging content on a wide range of topics, making complex concepts more accessible and enjoyable. They also provide opportunities to learn from experts and thought leaders, exposing you to new ideas and perspectives.

- **Seek** mentors who can provide wisdom and guidance and engage in peer-to-peer learning to gain diverse perspectives. Mentors offer valuable insights drawn from their experiences, helping you navigate challenges and make informed decisions. Their guidance can speed up your growth and provide a roadmap for success. Equally important is peer-to-peer learning, where you collaborate with colleagues and friends to exchange ideas and knowledge.

- **Engage** in activities that push you our of your comfort zone, such as public speaking, learning a new skill, or taking on challenging projects. These experiences not only stretch your capabilities, but also build confidence and resilience. By stepping outside of familiar boundaries, you confront and overcome fears, gaining valuable insights and skills.

- **Surround** yourself with a supportive community that encourages your personal growth journey and holds you accountable. Being part of a network of individuals who share your values and aspirations provides motivation, encouragement, and constructive feedback. This community can celebrate your achievements, offer guidance during challenges, and help you stay focused on your goals.

Each of these actions and experiences fosters new knowledge and usable skills. Cultivate a growth mindset by viewing everything you do as opportunities for growth and embracing challenges as learning situations. By integrating these practices into your life, you will increase your personal and professional capabilities while ensuring you remain competitive and fulfilled in any opportunity you have chosen to pursue.

SUCCESS MINDSET

Continuous learning and growth are key to your success throughout your life. Having a growth mindset is about seeing education and self-improvement as an ongoing journey, not just a destination. I encourage you to challenge yourself every day to learn something new, see obstacles as opportunities to grow stronger, and stay adaptable to embrace change because *that's where growth happens.* The most successful individuals are those who remain curious, seek knowledge from every experience, and surround themselves with people who inspire growth. Whether through books, mentors, or real-world challenges, every lesson shapes your path forward. Embrace the mindset that learning never stops, and you'll find yourself constantly evolving, achieving, and unlocking new levels of success.

Here are some suggestions to cultivate continuous learning and growth in your life:

1. Cultivate Self-Awareness
- Engage in regular self-reflection to understand your thoughts, emotions, and behaviors better. Use tools like journaling or personal assessments to gain deeper insights into yourself.

2. **Develop Emotional Intelligence**
   - Practice empathy, active listening, and effective communication to enhance your ability to understand and manage your emotions and those of others. Take part in workshops or read books on emotional intelligence.

3. **Incorporate Mindfulness Practices**
   - Integrate activities like meditation, yoga, or mindfulness exercises into your daily routine to improve focus, reduce stress, and enhance overall well-being.

4. **Engage in Therapy or Counseling**
   - Seek professional support through therapy or counseling to work through personal challenges, gain new perspectives, and strengthen your mental health.

5. **Prioritize Interpersonal Relationships**
   - Foster deeper connections with others by practicing active listening, showing empathy, and dedicating time to building and maintaining meaningful relationships.

6. **Strive for Balance and Holistic Growth**
   - Recognize the interconnectedness of personal and professional fulfillment by setting boundaries, prioritizing self-care, and seeking a harmonious balance between work and personal life.

Remember, success is not just about reaching a specific goal. It is also about the journey you take to get there. Focus on embracing a growth mindset that encourages within you resilience and creativity. Don't be scared to take calculated risks and learn from both your successes and failures. Remember to surround yourself with a supportive network of peers and mentors who challenge and inspire you. Your commitment to continuous learning and growth will not only set you apart in your career, but also enrich your life with meaningful experiences and achievements.

SUCCESS CODE:
CONTINUOUS DEVELOPMENT

Embrace lifelong learning, foster continual growth, seek diverse experiences, and thrive in change for success.

CHAPTER 11

THE FINANCIAL ACUITY CODE

Building Financial Security Empowers Freedom

And Long-Term Success.

S uccess is not just about having a steady income or splurging on the latest trends. It's also about financial stability that empowers you to live a life aligned with your values, dreams, and goals. Now, I know the temptation to spend impulsively is real, especially when you are young and the feeling of financial freedom seems just within reach. Trust me, I have been there. It's easy to get caught up in the rush of wanting to experience life and enjoy the present moment, but the trick is in finding the balance. It is about being a wise hustler and spending with intention, so that your money works for you instead of against you.

Financial stability is not just about how much money you have in the bank. It's about the choices you make with the money you have, ensuring that you are not just living for today but also setting yourself up for a bright future without unnecessary financial burdens. Whether you are navigating student loans, housing costs, or just figuring out how to save while still enjoying your life; there are ways to be strategic with your spending. Being financially stable gives you the freedom to make choices that align with your values, but true stability comes from understanding what matters most to you and managing your resources wisely. When you are in control of your finances, you are in control of your future, happiness, and opportunities. This code dives into the power of taking responsibility for your financial decisions and how that can shape a future with both security and fulfillment.

When I was working in that factory, I had a moment of realization that would change the course of my life. It was not just the long shifts or the repetitive tasks that wore me down; it was the awareness that I was stuck in a cycle that was not leading me anywhere exciting. I was not utilizing my potential, and I knew deep down that there was more I could be doing. I was just getting by, 'surviving rather than thriving.' The thought of spending the rest of my life in that same spot, in that same mindset, became unbearable. So, I asked myself one simple but profound question, *What do I need to do to change?*

That question became the beacon for a shift in how I viewed my finances and my future. Instead of letting my current circumstances dictate my future, I decided to invest in myself. I committed to my education, to learning new skills, and most importantly, to developing expertise in a field that I could really excel in. It was not just about the act of going back to school or taking courses; it was about the mindset of believing that I was worthy of more and that I could build something greater than where I was. I chose IT as my specialization, not because it was an easy route but because I was passionate about it and saw the potential for growth. This decision was an investment in my future, one that required time, effort, and *yes*, financial commitment.

Over time, the results were undeniable. As I deepened my expertise in IT, I began to stand out. What was once a job that seemed like a temporary solution evolved into a thriving career. I climbed the ranks, and soon enough, my skills became highly sought after. It was not just my company that valued me. Other organizations started to recognize my potential, and doors began to open. I went from being just another employee to becoming an indispensable part of any team I joined. This transformation was not purely about financial gain; it was about the fulfillment that came from doing something I was truly passionate about and thus, becoming a recognized expert in my field.

Looking back, the key lesson I learned was that investing in myself was not just about bettering my financial situation, it was about taking control of my future and aligning my passion with my profession. The magic of specializing in something that truly excites you is that it shifts the dynamics in your favor. It gives you the leverage to turn a job into a meaningful career, one that not only sustains you financially but also brings you joy and fulfillment. Financial stability came as a natural consequence of my growth and expertise. I was not just working to make ends meet anymore. I was creating a future and a legacy, one where I could live the life I envisioned. That's the power of investing in yourself.

In today's digital age, managing money has become more accessible through a variety of tools and resources. Mobile banking apps allow you to track spending, transfer funds, and pay bills instantly, and budgeting apps help you set financial goals, monitor expenses, and even automate savings. Online investment platforms make it easier than ever to grow wealth with minimal effort, while digital payment systems enable fast, cashless transactions. This can also feel overwhelming, especially for your generation who are juggling student debt, housing costs, and personal goals. The key to financial stability is not about making a huge salary, it's about being strategic with what you earn and knowing how to make your money work for you.

One of the most effective methods is using the 50/30/20 budgeting rule, which breaks your income into three categories: 50 percent for needs (rent, bills, groceries), 30 percent for wants (entertainment, dining out, travel), and 20 percent for savings and debt repayment. There are many apps available to track your spending and automatically allocate funds into these categories. These tools offer a clear picture of where your money is going and help create a financial plan that aligns with both short-term and long-term goals.

Consider the story of Anna, a millennial freelancer who is just starting to build her career. With an inconsistent income, Anna initially struggled with budgeting. After learning about the 50/30/20 rule, she started using an app to track her expenses and found ways to cut back on impulse spending. By focusing 20 percent of her income on paying down credit card debt and setting aside savings, she gradually built a safety net. As her income grew, she adjusted her budget to ensure she stayed on track while still treating herself to things she enjoyed.

Another example is Mike, a millennial with a family. He used a similar approach but had to adjust his percentages to prioritize his children's education fund and his growing mortgage. His experience highlights how budgeting can be flexible and depends on the unique needs and responsibilities in your life. Whether you are a freelancer, a parent, or someone starting a new job, these tools and strategies are adaptable to your situation, helping you stay financially responsible while balancing your personal values. By investing time in learning these strategies, you can build the foundation for lasting financial stability, regardless of where you start.

Financial acuity is not just about numbers. It is about the mindset you bring to money, the discipline to make smart financial choices, and the vision to build a future that aligns with your values. When you understand how to manage your finances strategically, you are not just surviving. You are creating freedom, stability, and long-term success.

Gratification is at our fingertips, and it is easy to fall into the trap of spending impulsively. Streaming subscriptions, daily coffee runs, and last-minute travel deals may seem small in the moment, but over time, they add up. Financial intelligence is about recognizing that every dollar you earn has power. The way you allocate it determines whether you are building toward security or setting yourself up for financial stress.

The key is balance. You do not have to deprive yourself of experiences, but you do need to be intentional. Setting financial goals, automating savings, and tracking expenses allow you to enjoy life today while securing your future. Small, consistent habits, whether investing in your education, diversifying income streams, or sticking to a budget, compound over time and lead to financial independence and peace of mind.

True success is not about how much you earn. It is about how well you manage what you have, how wisely you invest in yourself, and how intentionally you build a future that supports both your passions and your financial well-being. When you master financial acuity, you gain more than wealth. You gain freedom, the ability to live life on your terms, pursue your dreams, and create a legacy that lasts.

SUCCESS PRINCIPLE

Financial Acuity – To truly thrive, embracing this success principle in achieving financial stability goes beyond accumulating wealth; it is about making intentional choices that align with your values and long-term goals. Establishing a secure financial foundation requires thoughtful planning, such as creating and sticking to a budget, prioritizing savings, and avoiding impulsive spending. Financial acuity is also about investing in your future through education, retirement savings, and supporting causes you believe in. By reducing debt and preparing for unexpected expenses, you gain peace of mind, allowing you to pursue your dreams free from financial worry. These practices create a stable future while giving you the freedom to live with purpose.

To achieve financial stability, you must take proactive steps. Start by crafting a budget that reflects your income, values, and priorities, allocating funds for essentials, savings, and discretionary spending. Make sure to set clear financial goals and track your expenses to avoid unnecessary purchases. Consider investing in long-term financial growth, such as retirement accounts or diverse investment opportunities like stocks or bonds. Educate yourself on personal finance by seeking budgeting, investing, and debt management resources. Build an emergency fund to handle unforeseen expenses and focus on paying off high-interest debt to free up resources for future growth. These actions help lay the foundation for financial stability, enabling you to make empowered choices and achieve lasting success.

SUCCESS MINDSET

Achieving financial acuity is about building the right mindset, a blend of discipline, foresight, and resilience. As our future leaders, you need to embrace a mindset that sees money as a tool for creating opportunities, not just a means to fulfill immediate desires. This is where intentional financial habits come into play. It is not about being overly restrictive but about understanding the long-term impact of every financial decision. By adopting a proactive approach, you can understand the financial challenges and lay the groundwork for a secure, prosperous future.

Here are some actionable steps that can guide you toward financial stability:

1. **Create a Budget**
   - **Track Your Income and Expenses:** Use apps to track your spending and understand where your money goes each month.
   - **Follow the 50/30/20 Rule:** Allocate 50 percent of your income to needs, 30 percent to wants, and 20 percent to savings and debt repayment. Adjust these percentages to fit your unique financial situation, but this rule can serve as a strong foundation.
   - **Set Clear Financial Goals:** Break your goals down into short-term (e.g., building an emergency fund) and long-term (e.g., retirement savings) targets. Set deadlines to measure your progress.

2. Build an Emergency Fund

- **Start Small, Think Big:** Begin by setting aside a small percentage of your income, aiming to gradually build up to three to six months' worth of living expenses.

- **Prioritize Fund Building Over Extras:** Avoid spending on non-essentials until your emergency fund is solid. Consider cutting back on discretionary spending, like dining out or unnecessary shopping, to accelerate your savings.

3. Save Creatively

- **Co-Living:** If you are living in a high-cost area, explore co-living spaces where you can share rent and other living expenses.

- **House Hacking:** If you own a property, consider renting out rooms, a basement, or even a parking space to reduce your mortgage or rent payments. You can use sites like Airbnb™ to rent out rooms or properties for short-term stays.

- **Side Hustles:** Leverage your skills or hobbies to bring in additional income. Dedicate a portion of your side income to building savings.

4. Invest in Your Future

- **Start Retirement Savings Early:** Open a retirement account and take advantage of employer matches if available. Contribute regularly, even if it is a small amount to start with.

- **Diversify Investments:** Do not put all your eggs in one basket. Explore diverse investment options like stocks, bonds, crypto, mutual funds, and real estate.
- **Educate Yourself:** Invest in financial literacy. Read books like *Rich Dad Poor Dad* by Robert Kiyosaki or take free courses on personal finance to sharpen your money-management skills.

5. Reduce Debt

- **Pay Off High-Interest Debt First:** Focus on paying off high-interest debt, like credit cards, before tackling other debts.
- **Consolidate or Refinance Loans:** If you have multiple loans, consider consolidation or refinancing options, offering lower interest rates or better repayment terms. This can help you save on interest and simplify your payments.

6. Monitor Your Progress

- **Review Your Finances Regularly:** Set a monthly or quarterly reminder to review your financial progress, reassess your budget, and adjust savings goals. Ensure you stay on track with your plan and adjust as life circumstances change.
- **Celebrate Milestones:** When you hit major financial milestones, such as paying off a debt or reaching a savings goal, celebrate responsibly. Recognizing your progress keeps you motivated and focused on your long-term goals.

Financial acuity is more than just managing money. It is about cultivating a mindset of abundance, discipline, and intentionality. Every financial choice you make today shapes the opportunities you will have tomorrow. By budgeting wisely, investing in your future, and eliminating debt, you create financial stability and the freedom to pursue your passions without limitations.

True success is not measured by the number in your bank account. It is reflected in the choices that allow you to live with purpose, security, and peace of mind. When you take control of your finances, you take control of your future. You gain the ability to say *yes* to opportunities that align with your values and *no* to the stress of financial uncertainty.

The journey to financial independence starts with small, consistent steps. The more intentional you are with your resources, the more empowered you become. Wealth is not just about accumulation. It is about creating a life where your financial well-being supports your dreams rather than standing in the way of them.

SUCCESS CODE: **FINANCIAL MASTERY**

Master your money by planning, investing, growing wealth, staying disciplined, and creating freedom.

CHAPTER 12

THE ADAPTABILITY CODE

Gaining The Ability To Be Adaptive And Innovate
Through A Rapidly Evolving World.

In an era defined by digital transformation, you are part of a generation uniquely equipped to thrive. Growing up in a world that evolved from dial-up connections to the prevalence of smartphones and social media has given you an innate ability to embrace change and adapt effortlessly. Yet, the real challenge lies not in simply keeping up with this fast-paced evolution but in harnessing it to forge paths of personal growth, professional excellence, and meaningful contribution.

How you truly tap into the power of your adaptability is through tech fluency. Your journey through the digital age is one of unparalleled innovation and resilience. Unlike generations before, you do not merely adopt technology; you spearhead its movement by setting trends and redefining possibilities. You are the pioneers of social media revolutions, digital entrepreneurship, and remote collaborations. However, being tech-savvy and adaptable is more than just mastering the latest tools. It's about cultivating the confidence and wisdom to use technology as a force for good. This principle goes beyond skills; it's about recognizing the unique strength within you and aligning it with a greater purpose.

As you navigate the endless opportunities afforded by your adaptability, remember that balance is key. The ability to thrive in a fast-evolving technological landscape can be empowering but also feel overwhelming. By cultivating a growth mindset, embracing lifelong learning, and creating boundaries with technology, you can avoid burnout and ensure your adaptability remains a source of strength. Ultimately, your tech-savvy nature is more than a skill; it's a mindset that sees change as an opportunity to grow, innovate, and lead. This is your moment to 'take the bull by the horns' and shape a future that reflects your unique blend of ingenuity and adaptability.

Born in a different generation, I was not naturally immersed in the rapid technological advancements that define today's digital world, yet I understood early on that standing still was not an option. If I did not adapt, I risked being left behind and watching the world move forward without me. This realization ignited a determination within me to embrace change and push the boundaries of what I was used to. The journey was challenging. I had to educate myself, often starting from scratch, to understand and navigate the tools and platforms that were quickly becoming the backbone of modern communication and influence.

One of the most rewarding outcomes of this journey was launching my podcast, *Inspirational Journeys through Life with StraightTalkWith-Nolan.* Adapting to new technology gave me a platform to amplify my message and connect with people in ways I could never have imagined. Learning to record, edit, and produce episodes was a steep learning curve, but it was worth every moment of effort. Today, that podcast is recognized as one of the top twenty-five in South Africa, a testament to the power of adaptability and the willingness to embrace innovation. If I had not chosen to step out of my comfort zone and harness the opportunities technology offers, I would have missed out on this incredible avenue to inspire others and share my story.

Developing practical tech skills is essential for millennials to thrive personally and professionally. These skills can vary widely depending on their career paths, but certain ones are universally beneficial. For instance, mastering tools for data analysis, learning coding languages, or becoming proficient in project management software can open doors to new opportunities. I recall traveling internationally about a decade ago. When I got back, I advised my children to learn more about AI and data science. They did not pay attention to me at first, but now, they have chosen to learn it and are excelling in it. There are many platforms that offer free and affordable courses to help you build these skills, catering to various expertise levels. Whether you are in marketing, finance, or creative industries, understanding technology's role in your field positions you as a valuable, forward-thinking professional ready to tackle modern challenges.

However, being highly tech-savvy comes with its own set of challenges, particularly the risk of tech burnout. The constant connectivity, the pressure to stay updated, and the overwhelming flood of information can take a toll on your mental and emotional well-being. The dark side of technology often manifests as stress, fatigue, and even a sense of disconnection from the present moment. To combat this, strategies like digital detoxing, which is unplugging from devices for a designated period, can provide much-needed relief. Time management tools can also help structure your day and ensure you maintain focus and balance. Additionally, incorporating mindfulness practices, like meditation or journaling, can create a healthier relationship with technology while reducing the feeling of being perpetually 'on.'

For your generation, connecting with the concept of tech-savvy adaptability means leveraging technology to build both a successful career and a fulfilling life. This involves a conscious effort to integrate technology in ways that enhance your goals without letting it dictate your pace or priorities. By embracing lifelong learning, setting boundaries with tech, and staying aware of its potential downsides, you can unlock the full potential of your adaptability. Whether you are navigating new career opportunities, pursuing creative passions, or simply striving for balance, your ability to use technology wisely will set you apart in an ever-evolving digital landscape.

Adaptability is not just about keeping up with technology. It is about using it intentionally to shape a future that aligns with your values, ambitions, and well-being. While the digital world moves at an unprecedented pace, real success comes from balancing innovation with purpose, ensuring that technology remains a tool for empowerment rather than a source of overwhelm.

True adaptability goes beyond mastering the latest apps, trends, or coding languages. It requires a mindset of continuous learning, creative problem-solving, and resilience in the face of change. The most successful individuals are not just those who know how to use technology, but those who understand when and why to use it. They embrace its possibilities while remaining grounded in their vision for success.

This means finding ways to integrate technology into your life without allowing it to dictate your direction. It means using digital tools to amplify your career, enhance your creativity, and streamline productivity while also setting boundaries that protect your mental and emotional well-being. The real edge in the digital age is not just being tech-savvy. It is knowing how to adapt with intention, curiosity, and balance.

Your generation has an incredible opportunity to shape the future by adapting to technology and leading its evolution in meaningful ways. Whether through entrepreneurship, social impact, or personal growth, the key is to remain adaptable while staying true to your purpose. When you approach technology with wisdom and intentionality, you are not just keeping up with the world. You are actively creating the future.

SUCCESS PRINCIPLE

Adaptability - Being adaptable is not just a skill. It is a cornerstone of success in today's rapidly evolving digital world. Growing up amidst technological advancements has equipped you with the innate ability to embrace change and master new tools with ease. This principle underscores the importance of recognizing your natural proficiency with technology as a significant strength. By leveraging this advantage, you can solve complex problems, innovate, and capitalize on opportunities that others may find overwhelming. Your adaptability and tech fluency set you apart, enabling you to navigate the digital landscape with confidence and agility and making you an invaluable asset in any personal or professional endeavor.

To fully embrace this success principle, adopt a proactive approach to learning and growth. Continuously seek opportunities to enhance your expertise, stay updated on emerging trends, and creatively apply your skills. View technological advancements as opportunities to lead and innovate, rather than as challenges. This mindset fosters confidence and positions you as an innovator in your field. You can drive meaningful contributions and achieve lasting success in an ever-changing world by staying curious, open-minded, and intentional about your adaptability.

SUCCESS MINDSET

Adopting a reflective mindset rooted in being tech-savvy and adaptable empowers you in an ever-evolving digital landscape. Adaptability is about embracing a proactive approach to change, viewing emerging trends as opportunities rather than obstacles, and recognizing your ability to navigate this dynamic world as a powerful asset.

As millennials, embracing a success mindset centered around being adaptable means recognizing the unique advantage you hold in today's digital world. Your comfort with technology and your ability to quickly integrate new tools are powerful assets that can propel you forward. To fully leverage this advantage, start by staying curious and proactive in learning about emerging technologies and trends. View each new development as an opportunity to innovate and enhance your capabilities rather than a challenge. You can turn technological advancements into stepping stones for personal and professional growth by continuously updating your skills and being open to change.

Below are five actionable steps to help you create this mindset and stay ahead in this rapidly advancing environment:

1. **Stay Curious and Informed**
   - Dedicate time to learning about emerging technologies like AI, blockchain, and other disruptive innovations shaping the future.

- Follow industry news, subscribe to relevant newsletters, and explore learning platforms.
- Engage with tech communities or attend webinars to gain deeper insights and expand your knowledge.

2. Build Relevant Tech Skills

- Identify specific skills relevant to your career or interests, such as data analysis, project management software, coding, or design tools.
- Focus on practical applications of these skills, integrating them into your daily tasks to enhance efficiency and creativity.
- Consider certifications to validate your expertise, adding credibility to your professional profile.

3. Cultivate a Growth-Oriented Mindset

- Embrace change as a natural part of growth and view challenges as opportunities to learn.
- Reflect regularly on how you have successfully adapted in the past to build confidence in navigating future transitions.
- Set short-term and long-term goals to continuously upskill and stay motivated.

4. Balance Connectivity and Well-Being

- Manage tech burnout by setting boundaries for screen time and practicing mindfulness.

- Schedule regular digital detoxes to recharge and maintain a healthy balance between online and offline life.
- Use productivity tools to organize tasks and minimize information overload, ensuring you focus on what matters most.

5. Leverage Technology for Impact
- Use your tech-savviness to lead innovation, solve problems, and create meaningful solutions in your personal and professional life.
- Collaborate with others to share knowledge and ideas, fostering a culture of growth and creativity.
- Reflect on how technology can be a tool for personal success, social change, and environmental impact.

Adaptability is not just about responding to change. It is about anticipating it, shaping it, and thriving within it. The most successful individuals are not those who merely adjust to new technologies, but those who use them as stepping stones toward greater innovation, creativity, and impact.

True adaptability means blending technical skills with emotional intelligence, strategic thinking, and a deep understanding of your own goals. It is about knowing when to embrace new tools and when to step back, reflect, and ensure they align with your vision. In a world that never stops evolving, your greatest asset is not just your ability to keep up, but your ability to lead the way.

SUCCESS CODE: **DIGITAL RESILIENCE**

"

Adaptability and tech-savviness are your superpowers, so embrace them to lead, innovate, and thrive in the digital age.

HOW TO SUCCEED IN A MORE MEANINGFUL WAY

Embracing Innovation And Change Keeps You Ahead In
A Rapidly Evolving World.

You have now learned how to take the internal foundation you've built and apply it in powerful ways to the world around you. You've explored how to cultivate meaningful relationships, create balance in your career, adapt to change, and build financial stability. These aren't just tools for professional success but the building blocks of a life that align with your values and purpose.

The external world can often feel overwhelming, filled with challenges, expectations, and constant change. But you've seen in this section that success in the world isn't about fitting into a mold or chasing someone else's definition of achievement. It's about showing up, using your strengths, and creating opportunities that conform with your abilities. You've seen how connection, adaptability, and intentional action can transform your work and your entire life approach.

The truth is that success doesn't happen in isolation. It's not just about climbing the ladder or reaching personal milestones. It's *how* you engage with the people and communities around you. The relationships you build, the work environments you shape, and the contributions you make are all part of a larger journey toward fulfillment. You've now learned to navigate the external world clearly and purposefully. The codes you've just been shown will help you create the kind of success that includes others, makes you a lifelong learner, and puts people before profits. But there's still one more section on this wonderful thing we call success.

The next step is about *expanding your impact* beyond personal success. *How?* By stepping into leadership, creating change, and leaving a legacy that inspires others. True success goes beyond personal achievement and involves positively impacting others.

In the next section, we'll explore what it means to lead with authenticity, inspire transformation in others, and contribute to something greater than yourself. This is where your journey moves from personal success to collective impact, from thriving individually to making a difference in the world.

SUCCEEDING IN THE WORLD

Explore How Your Internal Work Meets Your Outer Life And
Realign Where Needed.

You've done the internal work. Now, you're applying it in your career, your relationships, and your community. But alignment doesn't stop at intention—it lives in your choices. Let's check in on how you're showing up. *Are you leading your day, or is it leading you? Are you choosing from fear or purpose?*

Your life is not meant to be squeezed into someone else's idea of success. It's intended to expand with your energy, your joy, your fire. Let's take stock and recalibrate.

Reflection Prompts:

· Where in my life do I feel most in flow? What supports that?

_____

_____

· What areas of my work or relationships need more balance or truth?

_____

_____

· How am I contributing to the world around me in a way that feels meaningful?

_____

_____

- What parts of the external world challenge me, and what do they teach me?

_____

_____

- In what ways am I using my voice, talents, or skills to create positive change?

_____

_____

Action Steps:

- Establish a boundary this week that honors your energy and well-being. What would that be?

_____

_____

- What is one way to serve others from a place of alignment?

_____

_____

- Write a "wins list" to track moments where you showed up as your best self.

_____

_____

- Make a list of mentors or peers you can connect with for honest feedback.

_____

_____

THREE

Your Expansion

LEADERSHIP, IMPACT, AND LEGACY

When Others Succeed, You Succeed,

Raising The Potential Of All.

A t this point, you've built a strong internal foundation and learned how to apply those principles to succeed in your personal and professional life. Success, however, doesn't stop there. True success isn't just about what you achieve for yourself; it's about how you use your growth to inspire others, lead with purpose, and create a lasting impact.

This is where your journey expands beyond personal fulfillment. You've mastered the tools to make change, and now it's time to step into a leadership role that influences the world around you. Leadership isn't reserved for CEOs, public figures, or people with grand titles. It's about how you show up in your community, relationships, and every opportunity you have to make a difference. In the everyday moments, you choose to uplift others, share your knowledge, and foster environments where others can succeed.

Consider people like Brittany Packnett and Reshma Saujani. Their legacies weren't built solely on personal success, but on their ability to transform their inner values into actions that changed the world. By co-founding Campaign Zero, Brittany Packnett, a fellow millennial, has dedicated her life to fighting for education and equal rights in the Black community. Reshma Saujani, the founder of Girls Who Code™, has empowered young women in tech and leadership, breaking down barriers much like Packnett has in education.

Leadership and impact aren't only stories from the past. Your generation is already leading change in powerful ways. Millennials are stepping up to challenge norms, drive innovation, and create movements that are shaping the future.

Rupi Kaur, a poet best known for her book *Milk and Honey,* uses her fame to advocate for gender equality and social justice. Through her poetry and activism, she empowers women to embrace their stories, reclaim their voices, and challenge societal expectations.

Meanwhile, in South Korea, BTS has dominated the global music industry and used their platform to promote mental health awareness, self-love, and charitable causes, proving that influence can extend far beyond entertainment. These individuals, from different backgrounds and cultures, demonstrate that success is not just about personal achievement but using one's platform to create lasting, meaningful change. Your platform, no matter how big or small, can create a meaningful, lasting impact.

In this section, you'll discover how to translate your personal success into meaningful leadership. You'll learn how to inspire transformation in others, redefine what leadership looks like going forward, and create a legacy that reflects your deepest values. This is about more than just reaching your goals; it's about leaving a mark that will inspire future generations.

Success isn't just measured by what you accomplish. It's measured by the impact you have on others. It's about creating opportunities, lifting people up, and contributing to a larger collective that succeeds because of your planted seeds. When you lead with purpose and authenticity, you don't just achieve success. You create a continuous effect that touches lives far beyond your own.

CHAPTER 13

THE EMBRACING CHANGE CODE

How You Pivot And Adapt Will Determine
How You Succeed.

As I reflect on the current era of dynamic transformation, I see a generation that does not just adapt to change; they lead it. Millennials stand as architects of a new way of living, shaping careers, lifestyles, and societal norms with unprecedented creativity and resilience. They have discarded the rigidity of tradition, embracing flexibility and purpose in their pursuits. This is a time of evolution where the ability to navigate change is not just a skill, it's a lifeline, a force that propels us toward reinvention and progress. Your willingness to embrace the unknown, question the status quo, and pioneer uncharted paths is redefining what it means to succeed in a rapidly evolving world.

Looking back at my own journey, I see parallels that resonate deeply with *having* to embrace change. Growing up in poverty, my life was defined by survival, questioning where my next meal would come from. But even amidst adversity, I realized one truth: I could choose to remain stuck in the poverty mindset or activate a spark within myself to embrace changes in my life. That decision to embrace something different from what I knew led me through a career as an IT professional, an international bestselling author, and a mindset coach impacting thousands. My story is proof that the willingness to evolve can shatter limitations and unlock boundless possibilities.

In this age of constant change, your power lies in your willingness to embrace it. You are not just spectators in a changing world. You are the innovators, the disruptors, and the dreamers shaping it. By questioning conventional norms and embracing change, you are carving out careers that align with your passions, advocating for causes that resonate with your values, and creating lifestyles that prioritize diversity and inclusivity. This is not without its challenges, it's a rollercoaster of uncertainty and exhilaration. But within change lies the beauty of evolution, the joy of forging new paths, the pride in contributing to societal progress, and the fulfillment of living with purpose. I respect the ever-changing world and by doing so; I allow change to change me for the better.

I will admit, in my younger years, even the mention of 'disruption' was taboo and often met with resistance or repercussions for even daring to challenge entrenched norms. Conversations with elders often felt like stepping into a time capsule, as their views were unshaken by decades of conditioning. As a fourth-generation Indian in South

Africa, I witnessed firsthand my family, like many others, holding on tightly to traditional ways and viewing change as a threat rather than an opportunity. Yet something within me rebelled against this rigidity. I realized that staying tethered to outdated mentalities would stifle my growth and my ability to contribute meaningfully to the world. So, I embarked on a journey of self-discovery, diving deep into my values, potential, and purpose. What I unearthed was a drive to evolve, not just for myself, but so I could also inspire and shift others.

My conviction for change was not easy. It was a path fraught with uncertainty, doubt, and the occasional pull of old conditioning, but the rewards became profound. As I realised my potential spurred on by change, I discovered the true meaning of success, aligning my actions with my values and serving humanity. Today, my foremost commitment is to leave a legacy built on love, progress, and the empowerment of others. Through my coaching, books, and social media platforms, I share this message of positive disruption and encourage others to challenge the status quo and embrace change as a motivator for transformation. Each step I have taken has reinforced my belief that we can collectively shape a future that values changing in the face of personal, communal, and global betterment.

What I see with your generation is an amplification of this drive to further disrupt and redefine old systems. In my coaching classes, I witness a generation that is unapologetically reshaping careers and lifestyles. They are prioritizing flexibility, purpose, and innovation and rejecting the rigid structures of the past. Whether it's the gig economy, remote work, or the entrepreneurial surge, you all are embracing change with remarkable agility. Your willingness to pivot, adapt, and leverage technology not only creates new opportunities but also challenges traditional work paradigms, inspiring a shift toward more meaningful and dynamic ways of living. This collective movement toward positive disruption reaffirms the power of embracing change, proving that it is not just a personal endeavor but a societal evolution.

You are a change maker, capable of redefining how we approach success and breaking away from traditional norms to create lifestyles that prioritize flexibility, purpose, and individuality. For example, look at the rise of digital nomads who blend work and travel by leveraging technology to earn a living while exploring the world. Gig economy workers are another testament to this shift, opting for freelance opportunities that allow them to tailor their careers to their passions and goals. Even unconventional family structures, such as co-living arrangements and shared parenting, reflect a broader commitment to redefining what it means to thrive in personal and professional life. These examples highlight how millennials are rejecting the rigidity of past generations, proving that success is no longer confined to a 9-to-5 job or a traditional family model, but is instead deeply personal and dynamic.

While the evolution of work and lifestyle offers unprecedented freedom and opportunity, it also calls for a new kind of resilience. The flexibility that makes these modern paths so appealing requires adaptability, as gig workers navigate shifting income streams and digital nomads design stability in unconventional ways. Rather than seeing these challenges as limitations, they can be viewed as invitations to grow, innovate, and redefine success on your own terms.

By cultivating balance and intentionality, you can shape a life that is both fulfilling and sustainable. Many are already embracing mindfulness practices like meditation, journaling, and digital detoxes to maintain clarity and well-being. Others are continuously investing in skills and education, ensuring they remain agile and ready to pivot as industries evolve. This ability to adapt is a strength, proving that reimagining success is not just about breaking away from traditional norms. Instead, it's about building a life that aligns with your passions, values, and long-term vision. Your commitment is a testament to what is possible when change is embraced and harnessed as a tool for growth and fulfillment.

EMBRACING CHANGE: YOUR TIME IS NOW

If there is one truth I have learned, it is that change is not something that happens to us, instead it is something we create. It is the force that propels us forward, the spark that ignites transformation, and the key to unlocking a life of purpose, freedom, and impact.

You are part of a generation that does not wait for permission to redefine success. You are architects of a new world, one where careers are built around passion, lifestyles reflect individuality, and impact is measured not by tradition but by innovation. You are proving that success is not a fixed destination but an evolving journey, one that bends, shifts, and expands in alignment with whom you are becoming.

Yes, change can be unpredictable. It can feel like standing at the edge of the unknown, unsure of what comes next. But here is what I know to be true: every great leader, every trailblazer, every visionary who has ever reshaped the world started in that exact place. They felt the fear and moved, anyway. They saw the uncertainty and stepped into it with conviction. They understood that growth comes from stepping beyond comfort and daring to evolve. I encourage you to embrace this moment. Welcome change not as something to endure but as the very thing that will shape you into the person you are meant to be. Stay bold in your dreams. Stay unwavering in your pursuit of something greater. And above all, trust yourself. The future is something you create, not something you wait for. And I have no doubt that you are creating something extraordinary.

SUCCESS PRINCIPLE

Embracing Change is the catalyst for personal and professional transformation. By adopting a mindset of adaptability, resilience, and continuous learning, you unlock new possibilities that extend far beyond traditional career paths. Whether stepping into entrepreneurship, leveraging technology, or forging unconventional opportunities, embracing change allows you to navigate uncertainty with confidence and purpose. Instead of fearing the unknown, you can see it as an open door, an invitation to evolve, innovate, and create a life that aligns with your aspirations.

Beyond individual success, embracing change is a powerful force in shaping society. It challenges outdated norms, redefines what fulfillment looks like, and fosters a world where inclusivity, sustainability, and well-being are prioritized. By using digital platforms to amplify diverse perspectives and advocate for meaningful progress, you contribute to a future where adaptability is not just a survival skill but a driver of innovation and positive change. When you fully embrace change, you do more than keep up with the world. You help shape its evolution.

SUCCESS MINDSET

To fully and happily embrace change, you need a success mindset rooted in adaptability, curiosity, and intentionality. This mindset invites you to view change as a gateway to personal and collective growth rather than a source of uncertainty. By adopting this attitude, you get to unlock opportunities to redefine success, align your actions with your values, and contribute meaningfully to the communities around you. The key lies in approaching challenges with resilience, exploring innovative solutions, and staying committed to lifelong learning.

To help you embody this mindset, here are five interactive exercises:

1. **Lifestyle Audit for Alignment**
   Reflect on your current lifestyle and identify areas that feel out of sync with your values or aspirations. Ask yourself:
   - *Are my daily habits aligned with my long-term goals?*
   - *What changes can I make to live more intentionally?*

   Action Step: Write down three small lifestyle adjustments you can make this week to better reflect your values, such as reducing screen time, prioritizing wellness, or exploring a new hobby.

2. Community Exploration Challenge

Join an online or local community that resonates with your interests or values. Whether it's a group for minimalists, digital nomads, or social justice advocates, immersing yourself in like-minded circles fosters connection and collaboration.

Action Step: Choose one community to engage with this month. Participate in discussions, attend meetups, or contribute your unique insights to build meaningful relationships.

3. Experiment with Flexible Living

Conduct a lifestyle experiment that challenges your routine and opens the door to new possibilities. Examples include adopting time-blocking techniques, trying remote work, or exploring minimalist living.

Reflection Prompt: After one week, journal about your experience. *What worked, what did not, and how did this experiment impact your mindset?*

4. Create a Vision of Adaptability

Visualize how embracing change can positively shape your future. Imagine yourself thriving in a world where you've adapted to evolving careers, societal shifts, and personal challenges.

Action Step: Draft a short vision statement describing your future self thriving in this adaptive lifestyle. Use this vision statement to inspire your daily choices.

5. **Commit to a Cause for Social Impact**

Identify a cause or issue you care deeply about and brainstorm ways to make a difference. Whether it's sustainability, mental health, or education; align your actions with your values.

Action Step: Take one tangible step to contribute, such as starting a fundraiser, volunteering your time, or raising awareness through social media.

Embracing change is not just about adjusting to new circumstances. It is about stepping into your power as an active creator of your own evolution. Every decision you make, every mindset shift you embrace, and every action you take brings you closer to the life you are meant to live. Change is not something to fear or resist. It is an opportunity to expand, innovate, and coordinate more deeply with your purpose. The more you lean into transformation with curiosity and courage, the more you will realize that every transition holds the potential for something extraordinary. The world is evolving, and so are you. Embrace it fully, and watch how life opens up in ways you never imagined.

SUCCESS CODE:
DRIVE TRANSFORMATION

"

Embrace change with resilience, innovate boldly, and shape the future you desire.

CHAPTER 14

THE LEADING WITH IMPACT CODE

How You Do One Thing Is How You Do Everything.

Choose To Make An Impact.

You are the generation standing boldly at the forefront of making a massive impact for the future, driven by a collective belief in a more inclusive, equitable, and sustainable world. Like climbers navigating uncharted peaks, you face resistance and unforeseen challenges, yet you press on with conviction, knowing that your actions today will shape a better tomorrow. Your generation's willingness to question outdated systems and advocate for progress is inspiring and revolutionary.

Impact is a tool for empowerment, guided by empathy and the desire to create a world where everyone matters. From fostering ethical leadership to revolutionizing community-driven solutions and redefining the future of education, your efforts reflect a deep understanding that meaningful progress begins with collective action. Digital platforms amplify your reach, turning grassroots ideas into global movements. You are not just reacting to change. You are leading it, proving that impact is possible when met with purpose and decisiveness.

This chapter is about recognizing the power of your leadership and the emotional maturity it demands. Leading change is not simply about intellect or strategy; it's about heart. It's about navigating the emotional terrain of passion, admiration, and hope and turning those emotions into fuel for impact. As you lead the change, remember that your energy, vision, and resolve are shaping the world around you and inspiring others to join in this vital journey toward creating a brighter, more impactful global unity.

As millennials, you are leading the charge in shaping profound societal transformations, embodying leadership that's both visionary and action-driven. Tech entrepreneurs like *Evan Spiegel* and *Brian Chesky* are prime examples of individuals who are reshaping industries and sparking innovation in ways that are making a lasting impact.

Evan Spiegel, co-founder of *Snapchat*, has revolutionized how we communicate and interact with content. By pioneering the concept of ephemeral messaging, he shifted the digital landscape, making communication more dynamic and authentic. Snapchat's influence goes beyond just messaging – it's also transformed how brands engage with younger audiences, how stories are shared, and how augmented reality is integrated into everyday life. Spiegel's leadership demonstrates how innovation in the tech space isn't just about creating new platforms, but also about reshaping the way people connect and experience the world.

Brian Chesky, co-founder of *Airbnb*™, disrupted the hospitality industry by reimagining how people travel and find accommodations. What started as a way to help people rent out their homes now spans the globe, connecting millions of hosts and guests. Chesky's leadership reflects how adaptability and bold thinking can turn an idea into a global phenomenon, transforming travel and giving people more affordable and personalized experiences. Through Airbnb, he created an entirely new economy of trust-based, peer-to-peer hospitality that empowers individuals to make extra income and travel more meaningfully.

These examples show how millennials are not only creating the technologies of tomorrow but also forging pathways for more inclusive, connected, and sustainable futures. Your leadership, just like theirs, proves that impact isn't just about technology itself – it's about how that technology can open doors and create new opportunities for people everywhere.

Today, leadership is no longer just about authority or decision-making. It is about leading with empathy, listening to diverse voices, and fostering inclusivity. Whether in social justice movements, corporate boardrooms, or the tech industry, millennial leaders recognize that

genuine impact is built on trust, compassion, and a deep understanding of the communities they serve. This people-first approach
strengthens relationships and fuels lasting change. In a constantly
evolving world, the most influential leaders lead with vision and
heart, proving that success is not just about what you achieve, but
how you inspire and uplift others along the way.

Being impactful requires more than just technical expertise or bold
ideas; it also requires emotional intelligence and a deep commitment
to shared humanity. Millennials who lead from a place of empathy
are reshaping how we think about leadership. Whether it's through
advocating for mental health awareness or creating diverse, inclusive
workplaces, they are making it clear that leadership is not a one-
size-fits-all model. Instead, it's about understanding, supporting,
and uplifting those around you. As a millennial leader, continue to
break barriers, redefine success, focus on emotional intelligence, and
ensure the changes you advocate for are sustainable and meaningful.

As you know from previous chapters, I am an avid adventurer who
thrives on extreme activities, often taking them on for causes close
to my heart. I have also shared that one of the most transformative
experiences in my life has been climbing Mount Kilimanjaro, an
adventure that extends far beyond the thrill of reaching its summit.
On each climb, I have witnessed firsthand the stark reality of climate change as the once-majestic tropical glaciers slowly disappear.
These glaciers that once blanketed the mountain now exist as fragile

remnants due to rising global temperatures. Their retreat is not just a distant environmental concern; it's a visible, urgent call to action. Standing on that mountain, I realized the importance of using my platform to raise awareness about climate change, combining my passion for adventure with advocacy to impact collective awareness.

My commitment to preserving our natural world does not end with hiking the mountains. I have also taken to mountain biking through the wilderness to raise awareness of rhino poaching, another pressing issue threatening our ecosystems' delicate balance. These rides symbolize the need to protect our planet's most vulnerable inhabitants, our animals. Each turn of the pedal represents a push for impacting ignorance, greed, and the destruction of our wildlife. I use my passion and hobbies to impact awareness for something others forget. Whether on Kilimanjaro's peak or the rugged trails of the wild, my dedication to giving back to society and addressing environmental challenges is how I lead with impact.

Every adventure I embark on is a powerful reminder of the interconnectedness of humanity and nature. Witnessing the shrinking glaciers of Kilimanjaro or the endangered rhinos in the wilderness motivates me to merge my personal passions with a greater, more impactful purpose. These experiences inspire me to raise awareness, fund initiatives, and advocate for our planet's preservation. Through these efforts, I aim to shine a light on critical environmental issues and empower others to join in the collective responsibility of safeguarding our shared home.

Leading with impact is using your passions, skills, and experiences to create meaningful change. True impact is measured by the actions we take, the voices we amplify, and the awareness we raise. It is about recognizing that every effort, no matter how small, contributes to a more significant movement. As you navigate your own path, consider how your passions can be a force for good. Find a way to connect with the world, witness its beauty and fragility, and take action where it is needed most.

As you journey through leadership and impact, remember the world changes by choice, not chance. The choice to lead with integrity. The choice to act with courage. The choice to rise. You have the power to shape the future, uplift others, and leave a lasting mark. So step forward boldly, knowing that your impact is measured by the lives you touch and the change you intentionally ignite.

UNLEASH YOUR INFLUENCE: LEADING WITH PURPOSE AND IMPACT

Leading with impact is not about waiting for the right moment or having all the answers. It is about choosing to step forward with courage and using your unique gifts to create meaningful change. You do not need a title to be a leader. True leadership comes from the way you show up, the way you inspire action, and the way you influence others through your words, your choices, and your vision.

Impact is not measured by the size of your audience but by the depth of your intention. No matter how small, every action you take contributes to something greater. Whether you are challenging outdated systems, advocating for what you believe in, or simply leading by example in your daily life, you are already making a difference. The world does not change through passive observation. It transforms when people like you step up, take action, and commit to shaping a future built on purpose, innovation, and integrity.

You have within you the ability to create something extraordinary. Your leadership is not about perfection. It is about persistence. It is about daring to push forward, even when the path is uncertain. It is about embracing the responsibility of using your voice, influence, and passion to uplift others and leave an undeniable mark on the world.

So move with intention. Speak with conviction. Lead with heart. The future is not something you wait for; it is something you create. And the world is ready for you to rise.

SUCCESS PRINCIPLE

Leading with Impact requires embracing adaptability, passion, and conviction. As impact enthusiasts, your drive to challenge old norms and push for real progress is evident. With your digital fluency and grassroots activism, you amplify marginalized voices and champion initiatives tackling major social and environmental issues. Your proactive approach combines empathy and innovation, making your commitment to reshaping systems for greater equity and well-being clear. Your willingness to embrace change highlights your leadership in driving this evolution and shows how you can turn digital and community-driven platforms into powerful catalysts for action.

Navigating this complex emotional landscape is essential as you balance your passion for impact with the practical challenges of advocacy. The sense of purpose and fulfillment that comes from making a difference is powerful, but it also brings emotional investment, especially as you face resistance and the pressure to innovate. Embracing impact with enthusiasm and a forward-thinking mindset enables you to transform your personal dedication into a collective force for societal improvement. By leading with both heart and action, you inspire others to focus on a more just and sustainable world, making your efforts impactful and a force for good.

SUCCESS MINDSET

Leading with impact is not just about the changes you create in the world; it is about how you show up in every moment, conversation, and decision. True leadership is not confined to grand gestures or massive movements. It is woven into how you carry yourself, the standards you uphold, and the energy you bring into every space you enter. Impact is not reserved for those with titles or platforms. It is a daily practice of integrity, vision, and action.

To lead with impact, you must develop a mindset that sees potential where others see limitations. You must recognize that influence is about inspiring others through your own commitment and example, not about control. Every challenge is an opportunity to innovate. Every interaction is a chance to uplift. Every idea has the power to spark something greater than itself.

The most influential leaders are those who understand that their mindset is their greatest asset. They do not wait for permission to create change. They embody it. They step forward confidently, knowing that real impact is not about being the loudest in the room but the most unwavering in their purpose. You are a force within this world, not just a participant. The only question is *how boldly will you step into that truth?*

Below are some interactive exercises to cultivate this mindset. I cannot reiterate the importance of this enough: make them a habit.

1. **Develop Resilience and Emotional Intelligence**
   - *Manage Stress and Emotions:* Advocacy can be emotionally taxing, so building resilience and maintaining your well-being is crucial.

2. **Balance Passion with Practicality**
   - *Be Strategic:* While passion is essential, pairing it with a strategic approach ensures that your efforts produce tangible outcomes.

3. **Cultivate Empathy and Inclusivity**
   - *Embrace Diversity:* Ensure that your efforts to lead societal change are inclusive and represent the voices of all affected communities.

4. **Measure Your Impact**
   - *Track Progress:* Success in societal change isn't always immediately visible, so measuring your impact over time is important.

5. Maintain a Long-Term Vision

- *Think Ahead:* Societal change often takes time. Keep your long-term vision in mind, even when progress seems slow.

Leading with impact is about showing up with intention, using your voice to create change, and turning your values into action. It is not about waiting for the perfect moment or the ideal circumstances; it is about stepping forward, leading with integrity, and inspiring others to do the same. The legacy you leave will not be measured by titles or accolades but by the lives you touch, the ideas you ignite, and the difference you make. So lead boldly, act with purpose, and remember that every effort can shape a better world.

SUCCESS CODE:
LEAD WITH IMPACT

Lead with passion,
protect with balance.

CHAPTER 15

THE IGNITING TRANSFORMATION CODE

Be The Beacon Of Light Others Need To

Rise In Their Success.

Igniting transformation means embracing the power of change as a driving force for personal and professional growth. This concept might resonate deeply, as it evokes a mix of excitement and apprehension. It can signify stepping out of your comfort zone and confronting the unknown with courage and curiosity. Embracing this *transformation code* involves a heartfelt commitment to evolving beyond old paradigms and cultivating an attitude that views change as a gateway to new opportunities. The emotional journey of this code is both exhilarating and challenging, as it requires letting go of past certainties and daring to shape a future that aligns with one's evolving passions and values.

The world is evolving rapidly, and to thrive, you must keep pace with the idea of constant transformations. My message to you is this: *Let change be the catalyst for your transformative journeys, personal growth, adaptation, and evolution.* Embracing change not only keeps you relevant but also propels you toward success. It opens doors to new opportunities and allows you to break free from limitations. By welcoming change with open arms, you navigate the complexities of modern life and also pave the way for a brighter, more fulfilling future for yourself and others.

You must cultivate a growth-oriented mindset through continuous learning and self-reflection to ignite transformation. Embrace change by seeking opportunities that challenge your perspectives and skills, whether through new projects, diverse experiences, or creative ventures. You can foster such resilience by viewing setbacks as learning experiences rather than failures and surrounding yourself with a supportive network that encourages and celebrates your growth. Leverage technology and innovative tools to stay informed and adaptable, and prioritize mental well-being to maintain a balanced approach to transformation. By integrating these practices, you can effectively navigate and thrive in an ever-evolving world, turning change into a powerful catalyst for personal and professional development.

Growing up in an era where technology was scarce, I did not fully grasp the power of adaptability until life experiences forced me to awaken this trait within myself. I used to be stubborn, content with the status quo, and resistant to change. Yet, I cannot solely attribute this behavior to myself. My parents instilled in me the belief that life revolved around securing a good education, financial stability, a decent job, marriage, children, a house, and a car, supposedly all marking the pinnacle of existence. *How times have changed.* Reflecting, I realize the importance of embracing change, evolving with the world, and understanding that true happiness lies in the journey, not just the destination.

My siblings and I were raised with admirable mindsets, yet the tools to unlock our creativity and innovation remained elusive and overshadowed by traditional education. Imagine a landscape where seeds of imaginative thinking and innovation lie dormant, awaiting cultivation. While we possessed knowledge, ingenuity, curiosity, and adaptability, the nurturing environment for these qualities often eluded us. The conventional educational system, adept at imparting knowledge and honing specific skills, sometimes neglected the cultivation of individual potential and exploration. The emphasis leaned toward conformity, neglecting the untapped realm of creative thinking and innovation. However, it's *never too late.* We realized our potential is boundless, awaiting ignition and channeling into transformative action. *This realization is why you hold this book today.* It's my gift to aid you in becoming your best self. I don't want you to settle. I want you to catalyze the change the world needs.

Back then, what I learned was about survival! Today, you have unlimited resources to do more than just survive.

When I was younger, I remember asking myself, *Am I really open to change?* At the time, I had no idea how powerful that question would become. It was more than just a fleeting thought. It was the catalyst for a journey of self-discovery that would shape my entire life. I did not realize then that my willingness to embrace change would determine how far I could go, how much I could grow, and how deeply I could transform.

At first, the idea of change felt overwhelming. It was easier to stay within the familiar, to follow the path I had always known, and to believe that stability equaled success. But the more I resisted change, the more I found myself stuck; stuck in routines that no longer served me, stuck in situations that felt uninspiring, and stuck in a mindset that limited my potential. The moment I truly embraced change, everything shifted. It was not always easy, but it was always worth it.

Looking back, I realize that transformation does not come from waiting for the perfect moment. It comes from being willing to evolve, even when it feels uncomfortable. Growth requires stepping into the unknown, taking risks, and trusting that you can adapt to whatever life presents. The world is constantly moving, and those who thrive are not the ones who resist change, but the ones who learn to harness it.

I used this mindset shift to propel myself toward my goals, and each challenge became an opportunity to learn, refine my vision, and become stronger. Change is not something to fear. It is something to embrace. It is the gateway to resilience, personal growth, and the kind of success that is measured by the depth of transformation you experience along the way.

Igniting transformation profoundly impacts how you experience and respond to life's challenges. This transformation fuels a sense of empowerment and agency, enabling you to approach obstacles with optimism and resilience. The emotional effect of this shift is a renewed sense of purpose and fulfillment as you recognize that your adaptability and growth mindset allow you to confidently navigate uncertainty. Embracing transformation also fosters a deep sense of connection to one's potential and the broader world, as you see yourself not as passive observers but as active creators of your destinies. This realization can increase motivation, engagement, and a heightened sense of personal and collective achievement.

The hallmark of your generation lies not just in your acceptance of change, but in your ability to wield it as a tool for nurturing innovative mindsets. Amidst the ever-evolving modern landscape, you must sharpen your mindset, turning challenges into opportunities and setbacks into stepping stones for growth and success. At the core of this adaptability lies a willingness to confront uncertainty and navigate life actively. Remember, *igniting transformation* isn't merely passive acceptance; it's an active engagement. For you, change is not a disruption but rather a catalyst for your growth.

IGNITE YOUR TRANSFORMATION: STEP BOLDLY INTO YOUR POWER

While our past education might have inadvertently overlooked the cultivation of our creative potential, the horizon ahead remains brimming with opportunities. It is an invitation to embrace our innate capacity for innovation, to break free from the confines of conventionality, and to chart a course toward a future where *igniting transformation* knows no bounds.

Transformation is not something that happens to you. It is something you create. It is the moment you decide to break free from old patterns, challenge the status quo, and become the person you are meant to become. You have already come so far, but your journey is just beginning. Everything you need to ignite transformation is within you: your courage, adaptability, and relentless desire to grow.

You were not made to settle. You were made to rise. The world is not asking you to fit into its outdated molds. It is waiting for you to redefine them. It is waiting for you to take your passion, vision, and unstoppable energy and turn it into something extraordinary. Every challenge you face is a stepping stone, not a barrier. Every shift, every pivot, every bold move forward is a testament to your ability to evolve.

So embrace change with open arms. Stand confidently in your power. Take risks, trust yourself, and move with purpose. The future is not written but shaped by those who dare to create it. And that creator is you.

SUCCESS PRINCIPLE

Igniting Transformation – Igniting transformation teaches us that embracing change is essential for sustained success and personal growth. Millennials have shown that success is about actively seeking and seizing opportunities for innovation and self-improvement that might not adhere to traditional paths. By viewing change as a catalyst rather than a threat, you can transform challenges into opportunities for advancement. This principle underscores the importance of maintaining a flexible mindset, where adaptability and continuous learning become integral to navigating the evolving landscape of modern life. The willingness to embrace new perspectives and technologies, which ignites a new sense of self, allows you to stay relevant and succeed in a world that is in constant evolution.

Igniting transformation reveals that success is deeply intertwined with purpose and inner willingness. This principle highlights the significance of pursuing endeavors that resonate personally and contribute positively to society. The emotional resilience built through navigating change fosters a sense of empowerment and confidence, driving you to overcome setbacks and persist in your pursuits. By integrating purpose-driven goals and cultivating enthusiasm for change, you can achieve a balanced and meaningful success that transcends traditional metrics.

Here are some practical success principles for embracing change and igniting transformation:

- **Redefine Comfort In Terms Of Growth**

  Rather than seeing comfort as a place of security, view it as a sign that you may have stopped growing. Challenge yourself to regularly step into situations that push your limits, whether that means taking on new responsibilities, learning a skill outside your field, or initiating conversations that challenge your perspective.

- **Turn Curiosity into a Habit**

  Transformation begins with a questioning mind. Instead of simply accepting things as they are, develop the habit of asking *why, how, and what if?* Read about industries outside your own, engage with people with different worldviews, and train yourself to approach the unknown with intrigue rather than hesitation.

- **Commit to Self-Renewal**

  Transformation is an ongoing process. Regularly reflect on your skills, habits, and mindset to identify areas for reinvention. Set aside time each month to assess what is working and what needs to change. This practice ensures that you are constantly evolving rather than remaining stagnant.

· **Embrace the Power of Temporary Discomfort**

Change often comes with discomfort, which is a sign of growth. When you feel uneasy about stepping into something new, remember that discomfort is temporary, but the rewards of transformation are lasting. Learn to sit with uncertainty instead of rushing back to familiarity.

· **Develop an Experimental Mindset**

Start experimenting instead of waiting for the 'right time' to act. Treat new ideas, skills, and ventures as test runs rather than high-stakes decisions. Trial and iteration will teach you more than endless planning ever could. Small experiments build confidence and pave the way for more significant transformations.

· **Align Change with Personal Values**

Transformation is most effective when it connects with your core values. When faced with change, ask yourself how it aligns with what truly matters to you. If you see change as a vehicle for strengthening your purpose, you will embrace it with enthusiasm rather than resistance.

- **Cultivate the Art of Letting Go**

  Transformation often requires releasing outdated habits, limiting beliefs, or even relationships that no longer serve your growth. Letting go is not about loss but about making space for something better. Regularly evaluate what you need to release to become a greater version of yourself.

- **Master the Skill of Adaptation**

  People often talk about adaptability as a trait, but it is actually a skill that can be honed. Develop the ability to pivot by practicing flexibility in small ways. Switch up routines, challenge your own opinions, and seek out unfamiliar experiences. The more you practice adaptation, the easier it becomes when major life changes arise.

These principles ensure that transformation is more than just a concept, it is an intentional and practical part of life.

SUCCESS MINDSET

Thriving in a world of constant change requires developing a mindset that views transformation as an opportunity rather than a setback. Approach challenges with adaptability and see them as moments to innovate, grow, and refine your skills. Curiosity is a powerful tool to embrace lifelong learning by exploring new ideas, perspectives, and experiences that push you beyond the familiar. True growth happens when you are willing to step into the unknown.

Aligning your work with your personal values and passions fuels both motivation and fulfillment. When your efforts reflect what truly matters to you, obstacles become lessons rather than limitations. Life is a continuous journey of growth and evolution, fueled by the desire to ignite transformation and unlock new possibilities. Every experience presents an opportunity to expand your knowledge, refine your vision, and step into your fullest potential. When you embrace change with excitement and curiosity, you open yourself to innovation, creativity, and boundless opportunities. True transformation happens when you confidently approach each moment, knowing that every step forward brings you closer to the life you are meant to create.

Integrating these principles into your daily life opens the door to continuous evolution. Instead of something to resist, change is a force to harness, guiding you toward a more meaningful and impactful future.

SUCCESS CODE: **TRANSFORM NOW**

Change is not a barrier
but a bridge to your transformation.

CHAPTER 16

THE ENTREPRENEURIAL SPIRIT CODE

Inventive, Innovative, And Inspiring Are The Cornerstone
Of Your Entrepreneurial Success.

Entrepreneurship is not just about starting a business. It is a way of thinking that transforms how you approach challenges, opportunities, and success itself. Whether you own a company, work a traditional job, or pursue a creative passion, having an entrepreneurial mindset allows you to see possibilities where others see limitations.

This mindset is built on innovation, adaptability, and resilience. It is about recognizing that setbacks are lessons, that risk is a necessary part of progress, and that success is created through intentional action. Entrepreneurs are not just business owners. They are problem-solvers, visionaries, and trailblazers who constantly seek new ways to grow, improve, and contribute. When you develop this mindset, you do not just react to change. You anticipate it, shape it, and use it to your advantage.

Traditional career paths are no longer the only option. Success requires thinking proactively, embracing opportunities, and challenging conventional norms. Having an entrepreneurial mindset means training yourself to see potential where others see obstacles. It means looking at industries, systems, and daily experiences with curiosity and possibility.

Think about the evolution of technology. The internet was once just an idea, yet today, it connects billions, drives industries, and has created limitless opportunities. Entrepreneurs are the people who saw that potential before it became a reality. They understood that the key to success is not waiting for opportunities but creating them.

The same principle applies to your life. Whether you want to start a business, advance in your career, or turn a passion into a profession, you must cultivate a mindset that seeks solutions, adapts to change, and remains open to learning.

Success is not reserved for a select few. It belongs to those who develop the habits and traits that set entrepreneurs apart. Resilience is essential. The path to success is rarely smooth. Challenges and failures will arise, but an entrepreneurial mindset sees them as stepping stones. Taking calculated risks is necessary for growth. You do not have to gamble everything, but you do have to be willing to step outside your comfort zone.

I learned this firsthand when I developed my online program. It was not just about creating content. I had to invest in video production, editing, visuals, and marketing without knowing if it would succeed. Before committing, I carefully assessed the potential risks and rewards. This is what entrepreneurs do. They do not just jump in blindly but also do not let fear stop them from taking action.

Entrepreneurs do not just follow trends. They create them. They see gaps in industries, system inefficiencies, and a community's unmet needs, then develop solutions that drive change. This is how new businesses, movements, and innovations are born. If you adopt this mindset, you will start approaching challenges differently. Instead of seeing obstacles, you will see opportunities. Instead of waiting for someone else to solve a problem, you will take the initiative to create the solution.

The world is changing at an unprecedented pace. Technology, markets, and industries evolve rapidly, and those who thrive are the ones who stay ahead of the curve. Entrepreneurs understand that learning never stops. They invest in personal development, stay informed about industry trends, and remain flexible when circumstances shift. They do not cling to old methods simply because they are familiar. Instead, they embrace change and use it as a tool for growth.

Entrepreneurs do not wait for the perfect moment or ideal conditions. They work with what they have and find ways to make things happen. They leverage available resources, build strong networks, and maximize opportunities that others overlook. Seizing opportunities requires action. It means recognizing when to pivot, when to ask for help, and when to trust your instincts. It also means protecting your ideas and ensuring your efforts are recognized.

I learned this lesson the hard way. Some ideas were stolen because I failed to secure legal protections early on. Now, I always ensure contracts are in place before sharing business concepts. This experience reinforced the importance of being proactive, prepared, and protective of your work.

I also learned this lesson when I embarked on a journey selling cosmetics, believing I could make a mark in the beauty industry. I was excited and determined, pouring time and effort into creating a brand that would bring joy and confidence to customers. However, despite my best efforts, the business did not take off as envisioned. The challenges were overwhelming, from fierce competition to shifting market trends.

But even as setbacks mounted, I refused to quit. Each obstacle became a lesson, and every failure a stepping stone. I learned about resilience, adaptability, and the importance of perseverance. The cosmetics business may not have succeeded, but it ignited something far more valuable, the realization that failures are not the end. They are lessons that push you forward.

Three Feet from Gold from *Think and Grow Rich* holds deep meaning for me because it reflects my own journey and the lessons I live by. Whenever I face tough moments, I remind myself that success is often just beyond the hardest struggles, and the key is to keep going.

I have encountered many obstacles in my life from growing up in poverty to surviving COVID pneumonia and even summiting Mount Kilimanjaro despite physical setbacks. There were moments when quitting would have been the easier choice, but I pushed through because I knew that my breakthrough could be just around the corner.

This story is a constant reminder that perseverance is everything. In my coaching, speaking, and programs like *Project One Million,* I share this lesson with others, encouraging them to keep moving forward, no matter how tough things get. Too many people give up when they are just three feet from gold.

Your potential is limitless. Whether you want to build a business, advance in your career, or make a difference in the world, having an entrepreneurial mindset will be your greatest asset. Success is not about waiting for opportunities to come to you. It is about developing the vision, resilience, and creativity to make them happen.

OWN YOUR FUTURE: THINK BIG, TAKE ACTION AND CREATE YOUR SUCCESS

The most substantial businesses, careers, and movements are built on collaboration, networking, and shared resources. Do not hesitate to connect with others, seek mentorship, and surround yourself with people who push you to grow. Most importantly, remember that entrepreneurship is not just about financial success. It is about impact. The most meaningful work comes from using your talents to solve real-world problems, whether in sustainability, healthcare, education, or social change.

By embracing this mindset, you are not just preparing for success. You are creating it. You are setting yourself up for a life of innovation, resilience, and purpose. So think big, take action, and build something extraordinary.

Entrepreneurial success is not about luck. It is about mindset. It is about the way you see opportunities, the way you adapt to challenges and the way you refuse to accept limitations. Whether you are starting a business, growing your career, or pursuing a passion, your ability to think like an entrepreneur will be the difference between waiting for success and creating it.

The world belongs to those who take initiative. The ones who see a gap and fill it. The ones who do not wait for permission but instead take bold action. Challenges will come, but they are not roadblocks. They are tests of your determination, your creativity, and your resilience. Every setback is a lesson. Every failure is feedback. The most successful people in the world are not the ones who never fell but the ones who always got back up.

Do not play small. Dream big. Take risks. Bet on yourself. Surround yourself with people who challenge and inspire you. Learn, grow, and, most importantly, act. The future is not waiting for you to be ready. It is waiting for you to take the first step.

SUCCESS PRINCIPLE

Entrepreneurial Spirit – To thrive in today's dynamic world, prioritize innovation, adaptability, and risk-taking in your career. Constantly seek creative solutions, think outside the box, and be original in your approach. Stay open to learning new skills and remain resilient in facing challenges. Embrace the flexibility and opportunities of freelancing, the gig economy, and remote work while recognizing the need to stand out by being more creative and integrating the latest technology into your ventures. Invest in continuous education, build a strong professional network, and utilize resources like incubators and co-working spaces for support and funding. Embrace failure as a learning opportunity, maintain a resilient mindset, and engage with your community for inspiration. Prioritize your mental and physical health to manage the stress of entrepreneurship. By committing to continuous growth and innovation, you can create something truly remarkable and seize opportunities to make a significant impact.

To navigate life with an entrepreneurial mindset, here are some practical, step-by-step success principles that can help you turn challenges into opportunities and ideas into reality:

Embrace Risk-Taking and Innovation - Understand that taking calculated risks is essential for innovation and success. Embracing uncertainty with a strategic approach can lead to breakthrough opportunities.

· Begin with small, manageable risks to build your confidence. For example, pitch a new idea at work or start a side project in an area you're passionate about.

· Learn from each risk you take, whether it succeeds or fails. Document your experiences, noting what worked and what didn't, to guide future decisions.

Develop Problem-Solving Skills - Entrepreneurs are often defined by their ability to solve problems creatively and efficiently. Cultivating strong problem-solving skills will help you navigate obstacles and find innovative solutions.

· Practice structured problem-solving techniques like *The Five Whys* or brainstorming sessions to explore multiple solutions to any given challenge.

The *Five Whys* is a root cause analysis method that helps identify the underlying cause of a problem by repeatedly asking *Why?* until the core issue is uncovered.

– **State the Problem Clearly**. e.g. "Our sales have dropped significantly this quarter."

– Ask *Why?* For example, "*Why* did our sales drop."

– **Possible Answer:** "Because we had fewer customer inquiries."

– Ask *Why?* again. "Why did we have fewer customer inquiries?"

- Possible Answer: "Because our online marketing campaign was ineffective."
- Ask *Why?* again. "Why was our marketing campaign ineffective?"
- Possible Answer: "Because we targeted the wrong audience."
- Ask *Why?* again. "Why did we target the wrong audience?"
- Possible Answer: "Because we did not analyze customer data properly."
- Ask *Why?* one more time. "Why didn't we analyze customer data properly?"
- Possible Answer: "Because we lack the right tools and expertise."
- Identify the root cause and implement solutions. In this case, the root cause is lack of tools and expertise in data analysis.
- Possible solutions: Invest in better analytics tools or hire a specialist.
- Engage in activities that require creative thinking, such as puzzles, strategy games, or hackathons. These can help you sharpen your problem-solving abilities in a fun and engaging way.

Network and Collaborate - Surrounding yourself with like-minded individuals can provide support, inspiration, and valuable resources. Networking and collaboration are crucial for entrepreneurial success.

- Attend industry events, join online communities, or participate in networking groups where you can connect with other entrepreneurs or professionals in your field.
- Collaborate on projects with peers or mentors. This expands your skill set and exposes you to new ideas and perspectives.

Practice Financial Literacy - An entrepreneurial mindset requires a strong understanding of financial management. Knowing how to budget, invest, and manage resources is crucial for turning ideas into successful ventures.

- Educate yourself on financial basics, such as budgeting, saving, and investing. Consider taking an online course or reading books on personal finance and entrepreneurship.
- Apply these principles in your daily life by creating a budget, tracking expenses, and setting aside funds for future investments or projects.

SUCCESS MINDSET

To excel in today's ever-changing landscape, it's crucial to cultivate a mindset centered around growth, creativity, and resilience. Embrace flexibility and explore various career opportunities, from freelancing to remote work, allowing you to pursue multiple interests and revenue streams. You must stand out in this competitive environment by adopting unique approaches and staying updated.

Continuous learning is essential. Invest time in online courses, workshops, and seminars to enhance your skills. Build a robust professional network by attending industry events and connecting with mentors who can offer valuable insights and support. Utilize incubators and co-working spaces to access the resources and funding necessary for your ventures.

Here are some suggestions on how to adopt an entrepreneurial spirit:

- **Invest in Continuous Education and Skill Development:** Take advantage of online courses, workshops, and seminars that focus on entrepreneurship and technology to stay updated with industry trends and enhance your skills.
- **Build a Strong Professional Network:** Attend industry conferences, connect with mentors, and seek valuable guidance and support. Engage with your local communities to identify issues that need innovative solutions.

- **Utilize Resources for Support and Funding:** Use resources like incubators, accelerators, and co-working spaces to get your startups' support and funding. This will provide a conducive environment for growth and collaboration.
- **Prioritize Mental and Physical Health:** Embrace failure as a learning opportunity and maintain a resilient mindset to handle setbacks. Prioritize your mental and physical health to manage the stress of entrepreneurship and maintain a healthy work-life balance.
- **Welcome Change and Innovation:** Continuously learn and experiment to stay adaptable and open to new ideas. Use creativity and technology to drive innovation in your projects and initiatives.
- **Cultivate a Balanced Life:** Ensure your life encompasses work, personal interests, and societal impact. Strive for a balance where professional success, personal fulfillment, and making a difference in society coexist harmoniously.

Lastly, view setbacks as opportunities to learn and grow stronger. Engage with your local community to find inspiration and address pressing issues with innovative solutions. Prioritize your well-being to manage the demands of entrepreneurship effectively. By committing to these practices, you can achieve remarkable success and make a meaningful impact.

SUCCESS CODE: **BE INNOVATIVE**

Embrace entrepreneurship, solve pressing issues, and persist with a 'never quit' attitude.

CHAPTER 17

THE EVOLUTION OF THE SUCCESS CODE

Be Open To The Ever-Changing Tides Of Success
And Be Willing To Ride Each Wave.

Amid ongoing technological advancements and changing social dynamics, the concept of success has expanded beyond traditional measures like wealth or status. Instead, it has evolved into something far more nuanced and deeply personal. My encounter with Thabiso, a bright and ambitious young man, highlighted this transformative perspective. Thabiso, like many of his peers, views success as a journey of purpose and authenticity, where fulfillment stems from meaningful contributions to society and alignment with one's values. His insights offered a window into a generation that values impact over individual achievement, collaboration over competition, and purpose over profit.

Thabiso was redefining success as an endpoint and a dynamic process. He measures success by the quality of his connections, his creativity in solving problems, and the legacy he will leave for others. This mindset signals a shift from conventional norms to a more holistic view of achievement, encompassing emotional well-being, inclusivity, and human evolution. Conversations like the one I had with Thabiso remind us of the power of listening and engaging directly with this new wave of thinkers. Understanding their values can foster environments that nurture their potential and celebrate their contributions to a better world.

This chapter is an invitation to embrace this evolving definition of success. It is a call to challenge old paradigms and adopt a mindset that values change, expansion, and taking action. It is about recognizing that success is no longer a solo endeavor but a collective pursuit, where each individual's unique gifts add value to the whole. As we explore these principles, let's remember that the evolution of success is not merely a trend, but a reflection of an individual ready to build a brighter and more inclusive future for everyone.

THABISO'S PERSPECTIVE ON SUCCESS

Thabiso Mogorosi, a remarkable twenty-seven-year-old leader and visionary, embodies the evolving mindset of millennial success. Our conversation revealed his profound belief in retaining childlike traits such as curiosity, imagination, and creativity, qualities he sees as the foundation for growth and innovation. Thabiso's insights reminded us of how adults often lose touch with these vital qualities, becoming consumed by the pressures of conventional adulthood. He shared how engaging with younger generations had deepened his understanding of their aspirations and inspired his journey of self-improvement.

Thabiso's dedication to continuous learning and change has been key to his achievements. He admits that many youths are unwilling to change. "Instead, we expect things to change around us. For the longest time, I have seen myself change and become the best version of myself, and I am not even close yet," he said. "This shapes my mindset. It is just respecting and valuing that change is of utmost importance in everything we do. Now, my mind is always on the verge of looking out for signs where I need to change. My mind still thinks like a five-year-old!"

Thabiso's definition of success is deeply personal and people-centric. For him, success transcends material wealth, focusing instead on positively impacting others and securing a legacy that benefits future generations. He dreams of creating a sustainable ecosystem in his province, where opportunities abound for the youth to thrive. His belief in the power of community and collaboration stood out most in our conversation. Thabiso reflected on his journey from humble beginnings to impactful leadership roles and credited his achievements to mentors, faith, and intentional action. His story of moving to Johannesburg with just 5,000 rands (USD $270.00) in his pocket to pursue his dreams is a testament to the power of determination and resilience.

Faith, visualization, and celebrating small wins underpin Thabiso's mindset tools. He emphasizes the importance of connecting with the right people, acting with intention, and leveraging the mind's power to visualize and create a desired future. His ability to draw inspiration from movies, books, and conversations highlights the value of introspection and open-mindedness. As he works toward building a supportive community for the youth in his province, Thabiso's journey is a powerful reminder that true success lies in empowering others, embracing change, and nurturing the qualities that keep our minds and hearts vibrant. I am inspired to witness how he continues to shape a brighter future for himself and those around him.

At twenty-five years old, success might look like establishing financial independence, traveling the world, or pursuing a creative passion. By thirty-five, priorities may shift toward career growth, starting a family, or creating a lasting impact in the community. As millennials approach forty-five, success might evolve to reflect a focus on legacy, financial stability, and mentoring the next generation. Thabiso Mogorosi's journey illustrates this beautifully; he has transitioned from engaging with youth and building technical skills, to now playing a pivotal leadership role in empowering his community. His story reminds us that adapting and redefining success is normal and necessary for growth.

Many of you feel pressured to 'have it all figured out' by a certain age, especially in a world dominated by social media where comparisons are inevitable. It is important to normalize the idea that success is not always a straight path. Instead, it's a journey filled with twists, setbacks, and detours. Thabiso's mindset tools, such as visualizing success and celebrating small wins, provide practical strategies to navigate this uncertainty. By focusing on progress rather than perfection, you can embrace your unique journeys and recognize that setbacks often lead to invaluable lessons and growth opportunities.

Your generation is also deeply aligned with the idea of purpose-driven success, emphasizing personal fulfillment and social impact. Thabiso's vision of creating an ecosystem in his province exemplifies this shift. Success is not solely measured by wealth or material possessions. Instead, success is measured by the ability to uplift others, contribute meaningfully to society, and leave a legacy. Millennials can connect to this concept by aligning their goals with their values and finding ways to contribute to their communities through volunteering, mentoring, or starting initiatives addressing pressing social issues.

REDEFINE SUCCESS:
YOUR JOURNEY, YOUR LEGACY

Success is not a fixed destination. It is a journey of growth, adaptation, and purpose. It evolves as you do, shifting with your experiences, aspirations, and the impact you choose to create. The most fulfilled people are not those who chase a single definition of success, but embrace its fluidity, allowing it to expand and transform alongside them.

You are not bound by outdated definitions of achievement. Your success is yours to define. Whether it is through building a career that aligns with your values, creating opportunities for others, or becoming the best version of yourself, every step forward is a victory. Comparison is the thief of joy, and social pressures will always try to dictate your path. Real success comes from tuning into your voice, honoring your unique journey, and trusting that every challenge, pivot, and lesson shapes something greater.

Embracing the unknown confidently allows you to move forward with clarity and purpose. Being open to change, committing to life-long learning, and continuously evolving your definition of success will lead to greater fulfillment. The world offers endless resources; books, podcasts, and online courses that can inspire and equip you to navigate change and uncertainty. Put your emphasis on curiosity and wonderment, remembering the importance of retaining a childlike perspective, which fosters innovation and creativity. By combining this mindset with intentional action and a willingness to adapt, you can continuously evolve your definition of success and achieve fulfillment in every stage of life.

The impact you create will be measured in accomplishments, the lives you touch, and the legacy you leave behind. Your success story is still being written. Make it one that reflects your truth, your growth, and your limitless potential.

SUCCESS PRINCIPLE

The Evolution of Success – The evolution of success highlights the power of maintaining childlike curiosity and embracing continuous personal growth. Creativity, imagination, and wonder—traits often overshadowed in adulthood, are essential for innovation, resilience, and fulfillment. True personal evolution encourages you to nurture these qualities, allowing you to approach challenges with fresh perspectives and adaptability. When curiosity remains at the heart of your journey, success is no longer just about reaching milestones. It becomes a lifelong process of learning, growing, and inspiring others along the way.

Equally crucial in self-evolution is the willingness to embrace change and view self-improvement as a cornerstone of success. A proactive mindset fosters resilience, determination, and the ability to learn from diverse experiences. By committing to growth, you elevate yourself and uplift those around you. True success is a balance between personal achievement and meaningful contribution. When you embrace this dual approach, you recognize that success is measured not just by external accomplishments, but by the depth of your transformation and the positive impact you create.

SUCCESS MINDSET

To embrace the evolution of success, your generation can adopt a reflective mindset emphasizing growth, legacy, and meaningful impact. Evolution demonstrates how nurturing curiosity, embracing change, and staying connected to one's values can lead to a fulfilling life. This approach encourages individuals to think beyond traditional markers of success like financial or career achievements and consider their actions' broader impact on themselves, their communities, and future generations.

Here are five steps you can do right now to align with this success mindset:

1. **Cultivate Childlike Curiosity**
   - Approach life with a sense of wonder and a willingness to learn. By rekindling the creativity and imagination often associated with youth, you can find innovative solutions to challenges and create new growth opportunities. Practice curiosity by asking questions, seeking new experiences, and exploring different perspectives.

2. **Embrace Change as Growth**
   - Recognize that change is a natural and necessary part of life. Instead of fearing uncertainty, view it as a chance to adapt and evolve. Reflect on past changes that led to personal growth, and remain open to new opportunities that align with your values and goals.

3. Define Your Legacy Beyond Career

· Success is not just about professional achievement, it's about the lasting impact you leave behind. Consider the relationships you nurture, your contributions to your community, and the personal growth you pursue. Regularly reflect on how your actions today align with the legacy you want to create.

4. Stay Connected to Your Roots

· Ground yourself in your origins, values, and the lessons that shaped you. This connection provides a strong foundation during challenging times and also serves as a reminder of your purpose. Thabiso emphasizes that staying true to your roots helps you maintain authenticity while striving for success.

5. Take Intentional Action

· Success requires more than dreams; it demands purposeful steps. Use visualization, prayer, and goal-setting tools to stay focused and motivated. Pair these practices with consistent actions that align with your aspirations and create momentum toward personal and community growth.

Success is not a fixed destination. Rather, it is a continuous growth, curiosity, and transformation journey. You unlock your full potential by embracing change, nurturing creativity, and remaining open to new experiences. True success is not just about personal achievements. It is about evolving in a way that inspires and uplifts others. Committing to lifelong learning and adaptability creates a legacy of innovation, constant growth, and meaningful impact.

SUCCESS CODE: **BE OPEN TO CHANGE**

Foster curiosity, embrace change, impact lives, and stay grounded.

CHAPTER 18

THE HONORABLE VALUES CODE

True Success Is Not Just About What You Achieve,
But How You Achieve It.

Success is often measured by what you do and even who you do it with, but the real measure of a person lies in the values a person exemplifies. The way you lead, treat others, and make decisions defines your success and impact on the world. Adhering to strong values is what separates those who achieve fleeting recognition from those who build legacies that last.

Values like integrity, empathy, accountability, respect, humility, and service are not just principles to follow. They are the foundation upon which great leaders and impactful individuals build their success. These values shape the way you make decisions, interact with others, and ultimately define the kind of leader you become. When your actions are aligned with something higher than personal gain, success is no longer just an achievement—it becomes a way of life seamlessly woven into everything you do.

Integrity ensures your success is built on trust and honesty, creating a reputation that withstands time and challenges. Empathy allows you to connect deeply with others, fostering relationships that are not transactional but transformational. Accountability keeps you grounded, pushing you to take responsibility for your actions and constantly strive for growth. Respect ensures that every interaction is rooted in dignity, valuing people for who they are, not for what they can offer you. Humility reminds you that success is never a solo journey and that learning from others will always keep you evolving. Service shifts your focus beyond self-interest, recognizing that true success is measured not just by what you gain and instead by what you give back to the world.

When you internalize these values, success is no longer something you chase. It becomes something you embody. It is reflected in how you handle challenges, treat others when no one is watching, and the legacy you leave behind. Living by these values means that your success is not just about reaching a goal but about ensuring that the journey to that goal is meaningful, ethical, and impactful. It transforms your work, leadership, and relationships into something greater than personal ambition. It becomes a force that uplifts, inspires, and sets a standard for others to follow.

I have always believed that leadership is more than just seeking recognition, it's about embodying the principles that inspire others. This belief was reinforced when I was honored with the *Ignite Leader of Change* award at the *Gatherama Gala* hosted in Las Vegas. This award was different from awards that celebrate financial success or business achievements. It was not given because of a single accomplishment or a milestone reached. It was a reflection of how I lead my life. It was about the values I uphold, how I treat people, and the example I set not because I sought recognition, but because I live in alignment with my core beliefs.

I did not campaign for this award. There was no application, no speech to persuade others why I deserved it. My peers, the people who worked alongside me, saw my actions, my consistency, and my leadership in everyday moments and chose to recognize it. This moment reinforced something I have always believed; success is not work when you live by your values; it is a natural outcome. Success is not something you have to chase; it finds you.

I have witnessed countless examples of individuals who achieved success quickly but lost it just as fast because they lacked integrity. They focused on results instead of relationships. They valued profit over people. But success without values is empty, and eventually, it crumbles.

Businesses define their core values to establish a clear foundation for operating, making decisions, and building company culture. These values act as guiding principles, shaping everything from leadership to customer relations. Yet, as individuals, we rarely take the time to define our own core values, even though they are just as essential in determining the direction of our lives.

Your *core values* are your internal compass, guiding your decisions, shaping your relationships, and ensuring that your actions align with the kind of person you want to be. Without defined values, it is easy to be swayed by external pressures, make choices that do not align with your deeper purpose, or compromise your integrity for short-term gains. However, when you are clear on what you stand for, you gain confidence in your choices and attract the right opportunities, people, and experiences that align with your vision.

Defining your core values means identifying the *non-negotiables* in your life, the principles you will never compromise, no matter the situation. They serve as a filter, helping you determine what is right for you and ensuring that the projects you take on, the people you surround yourself with, and the paths you pursue are in harmony with your beliefs.

YOUR VALUES ARE A REFLECTION OF YOU

When you know your values, you gain clarity in your decisions, attract the right opportunities, and create a life that aligns with your highest self. Your career becomes more fulfilling, your relationships become more meaningful, and your environment supports your growth. With a strong foundation of personal principles, you confidently navigate life and make choices that reflect your true purpose and lead to lasting success.

Your values shape everything from how you lead to how you handle challenges. They are the standards by which you hold yourself accountable. They dictate how you treat people, navigate difficult decisions, and respond to success and failure. They define what truly matters to you and help you avoid distractions that do not serve your purpose.

True success is built on trust, consistency, and ethical decision-making. Whether you are an entrepreneur, a professional, or a community leader, your values will determine how high you climb and how long you stay at the top.

SUCCESS PRINCIPLE

Honorable Values - If you look at the most respected leaders in history, they were not just successful; they stood for something. Their achievements were not just about personal gain but the impact they left behind. They led with conviction, staying true to their core beliefs even when faced with resistance. Their values were evident in every decision, shaping their leadership, work, and the lives of those they influenced.

If you want to build lasting success and leave a meaningful impact, you must first know what you stand for. Success without a foundation of values is temporary. It can be built quickly but can just as easily crumble. However, it becomes unshakable when success is rooted in integrity, purpose, and authenticity. It becomes a legacy, a contribution that extends far beyond personal achievement.

Standing for something greater than yourself means living and leading with clarity and consistency. It requires mirroring your actions with your principles and refusing to compromise them for short-term gains. It is making decisions that reflect your identity rather than simply what is most convenient or profitable. Leaders who stand for something do not wait for external validation. They define success on their own terms, guided by an internal compass of integrity and purpose.

Here are the core values that will shape your success and define your legacy:

1. **Integrity: The Foundation of Trust**
   - Integrity means doing what is right even when no one is watching. It is about honesty, transparency, and unwavering in your ethics, whether in business, leadership, or personal relationships.
   - People with integrity do not cut corners for quick gains. They do not compromise their values for short-term success. They build trust by staying true to their word, making fair decisions, and treating others with respect.

2. **Empathy: The Ability to Connect and Lead**
   - Success is not just about what you achieve for yourself. It is also about how you uplift others along the way. Empathy allows you to understand the perspectives of those around you, creating stronger relationships and deeper trust.
   - A leader without empathy may reach success, but they will not keep it. People follow those who genuinely care about their well-being, listen, and lead with understanding rather than ego.

3. **Accountability: Owning Your Actions and Choices**
   - There is no true success without accountability. Taking responsibility for your actions, mistakes, and decisions separates leaders from those who make excuses.

- Accountability means showing up consistently, following through on commitments, and acknowledging when you have fallen short. It means being someone others can rely on, knowing you will take ownership of your role in every situation.

4. Respect: How You Treat Others Defines You

- Respect is not just about being polite. It is about honoring others' time, contributions, and perspectives, regardless of their status or background.
- The most successful people understand that respect creates opportunities. It fosters loyalty, strengthens teams, and opens doors to collaborations that would not exist in an environment of arrogance or dismissiveness.

5. Humility: Success Is Never Just About You

- Humility is recognizing that no one achieves success alone. It is understanding that there is always more to learn, that mistakes are part of the process, and that your success reflects the people who have helped you along the way.
- True leaders do not let their egos get in the way of growth. They listen, adapt, and remain open to feedback. They recognize that every person they meet has something to teach them.

6. Service: Success Means Giving Back

- The highest level of success is about how much you give, rather than just personal gain. Those who make a lasting impact understand that success should be used as a tool for service, whether through mentorship, philanthropy, or simply making decisions that benefit more than just themselves.
- Service-oriented success means asking, *"How can I use what I have built to help others?"* It means lifting others as you climb, creating opportunities, and using your platform to drive positive change.

Living by strong values does not just make you a better leader; it makes you a person others' trust, respect, and want to follow. It ensures that the success you build is not temporary, but it becomes a lasting legacy.

SUCCESS MINDSET

To truly embody this principle, take the time to reflect on your own core values. *What do you believe in? What are the non-negotiables in your life and career? What do you want to be remembered for?* Success is not just about reaching goals, but ensuring that your path aligns with the person you want to be.

When you stand for something, you build trust. You create a reputation that lasts. You inspire others to do the same. And most importantly, you build a success story that is not just about achievement but about real impact, meaningful leadership, and a legacy that endures.

To build a life of integrity, purpose, and fulfillment, you must first define what values are most important to you. Here is a simple way to start:

1. **Reflect on What Matters Most**
    - *What principles guide your decisions?*
    - *What kind of person do you want to be remembered as?*
    - *What qualities do you admire in others?*

2. **Identify Your Non-Negotiables**
    - *What are the things you will never compromise?*
    - *What lines will you never cross, no matter the reward?*

3. Align Your Life with These Values

- *Are your daily actions and decisions reflective of your core values?*
- *Are you surrounding yourself with people who share or respect your values?*

When you take the time to define your personal core values, you create a strong foundation for success. You gain clarity in your decisions, build deeper trust in yourself, and attract opportunities that align with your purpose. More importantly, you ensure that your success is not just about achievement but about achieving things in a way that resonates with the person you truly are.

Incorporating values into your daily life does not require grand gestures. It happens in the small choices you make every day.

- *Are your decisions rooted in integrity?* Ask yourself, "Am I making choices that harmonize with my highest principles, even when no one is watching?"
- *How do you lead with empathy?* Ask yourself, "Am I treating people with kindness and respect, fostering trust and loyalty in my relationships?"
- *Do you hold yourself accountable?* Ask yourself, "Am I owning my mistakes, learning from them, and consistently striving to improve?"
- By making these questions a daily practice, you ensure that your actions reflect the values you stand for, creating a foundation for success built on authenticity and purpose.

SUCCESS CODE:
HONOR YOUR VALUES

Success built on values is not just about what you accomplish. It is about how people remember you, not just for what you did, but for how you did it.

CHAPTER 19

FOSTERING UNITY CODE

Unity Is The Key To Creating A Better World For
All To Enjoy And Succeed In.

If you take from this book one overarching principle, I hope it will be that *success is not a solo pursuit.* The most meaningful accomplishments are built through collaboration, shared vision, and the ability to bring people together. Unity is the foundation of progress, whether in business, leadership, or society at large. The force turns ideas into movements, small actions into global change, and individual success into something far greater.

I know this truth personally.

Growing up in South Africa during a time of profound racial division, I did not have the luxury of believing in unity. I was born into a world where my skin color dictated my opportunities, where laws determined where I could go, and what I could do. Apartheid was not just a political system; It was a daily reality that told me I was less than, that I did not belong, and that I had to work twice as hard just to be seen.

One of the moments that shaped my understanding of division happened during my school years. In South Africa, under Apartheid, schools were not just places of learning. They were symbols of segregation. The system was designed so that children of different races did not receive the same education, resources, or opportunities. The schools for white students were well-funded, had modern facilities, and offered a wealth of academic and extracurricular opportunities. The schools for students of color, like mine, were under-funded, overcrowded, and stripped of resources.

I remember walking past a school meant for white children on my way home. Their playgrounds were filled with equipment, their classrooms had new textbooks, and their uniforms were crisp. I would look down at my own tattered school books, handed down year after year, and wonder why my education was considered less important. But even more than the physical differences, the unspoken message left an impact. The message was that *some people mattered more than others. Some were entitled to opportunities, while others had to fight for scraps.*

That moment planted a seed in me. I promised myself that I would never let a system define my worth. That I would become someone who created opportunities, not just for myself but for others. I did not just want to succeed. I wanted to prove that success should never be determined by race, background, or social class. I have carried that promise with me my entire life. I have used every platform, every business, and every conversation to push for unity, opportunity, and equality for all.

I am grateful to have lived long enough to see the change I once thought was impossible. I have watched a world that once divided people by race, gender, and identity move toward something greater. And while there is still work to be done, I know that millennials are the generation that will lead the charge.

The world's greatest advancements, whether in technology, medicine, human rights, or business, were not achieved in isolation. They were the result of people coming together with a shared mission.

Unity is more than just working together. It is the conscious act of uplifting one another, recognizing that our collective success is tied to how well we support and empower those around us. True unity is not passive. It is intentional. It is the willingness to break down barriers, listen, collaborate, and build bridges between people of different backgrounds, experiences, and perspectives.

Unity is about more than just coexistence. It is about thriving together, looking beyond our differences, and recognizing our shared humanity. It consists of seeing competition replaced with collaboration, division replaced with dialogue, and exclusion replaced with opportunity. Unity at the core of leadership, business, and social progress fosters innovation, inclusion, and long-term success; it transforms industries and even societies.

One of modern history's most powerful displays of unity has been the rise of social justice movements that have transcended borders. Millennials have been at the forefront of movements such as *Black Lives Matter,* climate action protests, and gender equality initiatives. They are using social media and digital platforms to amplify voices, organize global protests, and demand systemic change. These movements have proven that when people stand together, regardless of their race, nationality, or background, they can hold the most powerful institutions accountable and reshape policies that once seemed immovable.

In the last two decades, the fight for LGBTQ+ rights has been one of the most significant examples of unity driving change. Countries around the world, including the United States, South Africa, Canada, and the UK, have seen the legalization of same-sex marriage, a milestone achieved through years of advocacy, solidarity, and collective action. This victory was not just about one community fighting alone. It was made possible by allies standing alongside LGBTQ+ individuals, businesses advocating for workplace equality, and leaders willing to challenge outdated laws. It is a testament to how, when unity prevails, barriers that once seemed impossible to break come crashing down.

The COVID-19 pandemic revealed the power of unity in times of crisis. Scientists, researchers, and healthcare professionals from around the world came together to develop vaccines at an unprecedented speed, share critical data, and aid the most vulnerable communities. Beyond science, solidarity was seen in how neighbors helped one another, communities rallied around small businesses, and people found new ways to stay connected despite being physically apart. It was a reminder that our survival and success are deeply intertwined and that collective action is what carries us through our toughest challenges.

Millennials have reshaped how businesses operate by demanding excellent representation, inclusion, and ethical leadership. Corporations that once thrived on exclusivity are now implementing diversity initiatives, creating more inclusive hiring practices, and ensuring that leadership reflects our diverse world. This shift did not happen because one person spoke out. It happened because millions of individuals unified their voices, refusing to work for or support companies that did not reflect their values.

MAKING YOUR MARK IN YOUR JOURNEY

As someone who was once told that my skin color determined my opportunities, I never imagined I would witness the kind of progress I see today. I have lived through segregation, but I have also lived through transformation. I have seen doors that were once closed swing open. I have witnessed voices that were once silenced rise in unison. I have seen how when people unite around a common cause; they change more than just policy. They also change the course of history.

And now, it is your turn.

You and your generation have the most powerful tools at your fingertips to unite people, dismantle division, and build something greater than any individual could. The future is shaped by those who dream of a better world and those who work together to create it.

Success, fulfillment, and progress are never meant to be solitary. True success is measured by what you contribute to the collective good, not by what you accomplish alone.

Unity is not just an idea. It is the foundation of everything great that has ever been achieved.

SUCCESS PRINCIPLE

Fostering Unity is about recognizing that true success is never achieved in isolation. The most enduring accomplishments are built on collaboration, shared vision, and the ability to uplift those around you. Unity is the force that turns ideas into movements, obstacles into opportunities, and individual success into something far greater.

When you embrace unity, you unlock the power of collective action. You create spaces where diversity is celebrated, all voices are heard, and progress is fueled by inclusion rather than division. The leaders who leave lasting legacies are those who understand that success is about more than what you achieve. It's how you contribute to the world around you.

Unity does not mean agreement on everything. It means respecting differences, finding common ground, and working toward a greater purpose. By fostering connection, practicing empathy, and leading with integrity, you amplify your impact in ways you could never accomplish alone. When you commit to unification, you do not just build a better future for yourself—you build it for everyone.

If you want to achieve something extraordinary, find ways to collaborate. If you're going to build a meaningful career, align yourself with those who share your vision. If you want to create a lasting impact, lead with unity, not division.

Here are key ways to embrace unity in your own life:

- **Build Bridges, Not Barriers:** Be intentional about forming relationships with people from different backgrounds, industries, and perspectives. The greatest ideas often come from unexpected places.
- **Lead with a Spirit of Togetherness:** Leadership is not about being the loudest voice in the room. It is about creating environments where everyone feels seen, heard, and valued.
- **Champion Collective Success:** Celebrate the wins of others as much as you celebrate your own. Success is a collaboration, not a competition.

SUCCESS MINDSET

Your strength comes from embracing diverse perspectives, seeking new viewpoints, and truly listening to others. When you approach the world with curiosity and openness, you create an environment where dialogue thrives, respect deepens, and innovation flourishes. Welcoming different voices challenges assumptions, uncovers blind spots, and strengthens problem-solving by drawing on collective wisdom. By fostering inclusivity in your conversations, decisions, and actions, you expand your understanding, build stronger connections, and open the door for groundbreaking ideas to take shape. Unity in thought does not mean uniformity. It means creating space for growth, collaboration, and transformative progress.

Here are some suggestions on how to create more unity in your life and community:

1. **Lead with Inclusion:** Actively seek out and amplify voices that are different from your own. Whether in the workplace, social settings, or personal conversations, consciously listen, learn, and include.

2. **Encourage Collaborative Growth:** Support mentorship and knowledge-sharing, especially across different backgrounds and industries. When people from diverse experiences come together, innovation thrives, and new opportunities emerge.

3. **Create Bridges, Not Barriers:** Challenge biases, both your own and those embedded in the systems around you. Speak up when you see exclusion, and advocate for fair and inclusive hiring, education, and leadership practices.

4. **Embrace Cultural Awareness:** Engage with different traditions, perspectives, and worldviews. Attend cultural events, read books from diverse authors, and have conversations that expand your understanding of people outside your own lived experience.

5. **Strengthen Your Community:** Get involved in initiatives that bring people together, whether through volunteer work, community events, or supporting causes that promote equity and inclusion. Even small actions, like introducing people who might benefit from knowing each other, help foster a sense of connection.

6. **Champion Workplace Inclusivity:** Encourage diverse hiring practices, participate in inclusion-driven programs, and advocate for policies that create fair opportunities for all. A truly unified workplace values every voice and ensures all contributions are recognized.

7. **Celebrate Shared Humanity:** Unity is not about erasing differences. It is about recognizing that at our core we all seek respect, belonging, and opportunity. By approaching life with an open heart and a willingness to connect, you create ripple effects of change that extend beyond yourself.

True progress is built when people come together with a shared purpose. Embracing unity means recognizing that we are stronger when we uplift one another, respect different perspectives, and work toward a common goal. Success is not just about individual achievement, it is also about the collective impact we create when we foster connection, collaboration, and inclusion.

By choosing unity over division and collaboration over isolation, you accelerate your own success while also contributing to a world where progress is sustainable, voices are amplified, and possibilities are limitless. Authentic leadership is not about standing alone at the top but bringing others with you and creating a legacy of inclusivity, strength, and shared success.

SUCCESS CODE: **FOSTERING DIVERSITY**

Unite with purpose, embrace
diversity and uplift others.

CHAPTER 20

THE BEING TRUE TO YOU CODE

Authenticity Is Your Greatest Superpower. When You Live In
Alignment With Your True Self, Success Follows Naturally.

Throughout this journey, we have explored the principles of success, adaptability, leadership, impact, and transformation. But all of it, every single code, every mindset shift, every strategy, means nothing if it is not built upon a foundation of authenticity.

If you take away only one thing from this book, let it be this: *who you are at your core is already enough.* This is one of the most important codes that I have shared with you.

Authenticity is more than just about being yourself. It is also about choosing to be yourself in every aspect of life, including your career, your relationships, your leadership, and your vision for the future. It is about removing the mask, rejecting external pressures, and showing up in the world as the person you were always meant to be.

So many people chase success by trying to fit into someone else's mold, but true success is only possible when you stop performing and start owning who you are. Many people live their lives trying to fit into an expectation never meant for them. They choose careers, relationships, and lifestyles that do not align with who they are simply because they fear stepping outside the norm.

Throughout my journey, I have seen how embracing authenticity transforms lives. I have coached people who left high-paying but soul-draining jobs to start businesses that aligned with their passions. I have watched people overcome self-doubt by sharing their truth and inspiring others. I have seen individuals step away from the pressure to conform and build lives that reflect their deepest values instead. Whenever someone chooses authenticity over expectation, they unlock a new level of freedom and fulfillment that cannot be found in external validation alone.

When you embrace authenticity, you become magnetic. Opportunities align because you are no longer forcing yourself into spaces that do not fit. Instead, you naturally attract the right people, projects, and experiences that resonate with who you truly are. You stop chasing approval and start allowing success to unfold in organic and aligned ways. The doors that once seemed closed begin to open effortlessly because you are no longer trying to be someone you are not.

Relationships deepen because authenticity fosters genuine connection. When you show up as your true self, you invite others to do the same. The walls of pretense come down, and the relationships you cultivate are built on trust, respect, and mutual understanding. People are drawn to those who are unapologetically themselves because authenticity creates a sense of safety and relatability that strengthens both personal and professional bonds.

Success becomes inevitable because when you live in alignment with your truth, you operate from a place of confidence, clarity, and purpose. You stop wasting energy on maintaining a facade and instead channel that energy into meaningful work that excites and fulfills you. You make decisions with certainty, knowing they reflect your values rather than external expectations. Every step forward feels right because you are no longer walking a path designed by someone else. Instead, you are creating your own.

Your authenticity is your greatest asset. It is the key to unlocking external achievements and a life of purpose, passion, and fulfillment. When you embrace who you truly are, you no longer measure success solely by titles, income, or recognition. Instead, success becomes about waking up every day feeling coordinated, inspired, and deeply connected to the work you do and the life you live. It becomes about knowing that you are making an impact not by trying to be someone else, but by fully stepping into the person you were always meant to be.

When I failed my grade twelve exams, I felt like my future had been ripped away from me. For years, I let that failure define me. I kept my ambitions small, afraid to reach too high or want too much. I convinced myself that success belonged to others, to those who had the right grades, the right background, or the right opportunities. I thought my path had already been determined, which did not lead to anything extraordinary.

But deep inside, I knew I was meant for more. A fire inside me refused to go out, even when doubt tried to smother it. I began to question the limits I had placed on myself. *Were they real, or had I accepted them because of fear?* Everything changed when I stopped running from my story and started owning it. I realized that failure was not a life sentence. It was a lesson, a turning point, a chance to rise stronger than before.

The more I embraced my truth, the more doors opened. The more I trusted my path, the more aligned I became with the success that was meant for me. I stopped trying to fit into a version of success that was not mine and started creating my own. I found purpose in helping others do the same, showing them that their past does not define their future. Who you are authentically is who everyone wants to be with, because when you live authentically, you give others permission to do the same.

THE BEST SUCCESS IS YOU BEING YOU

Authenticity is not just a feel-good concept. It is the life force for success. It gives you the courage to take bold steps, the resilience to overcome obstacles, and the confidence to walk your own path. When you embrace who you truly are, you remove the limitations that once held you back and step into a fearless, purpose-driven, and unstoppable version of yourself. Success is not about fitting into a mold or following a predetermined path. It is about standing firmly in yourself, owning your journey, showing up in the world as your most authentic self, and becoming more of who you are. Aligning with your values, trusting your instincts, and leading with your heart..

I know what it feels like to doubt yourself, wonder if you are enough, and battle the fear that if you fully embrace who you are, you might not be accepted. I have been there. I spent years chasing external validation, believing success was about proving myself to others. But I learned that genuine success is not about outward appreciation. It is about finding your true worth and knowing your greatest value is what you foster from within.

You do not have to be perfect. You do not have to have it all figured out. But you *do* have to be real. Because the world does not need another imitation. It needs you, fully, unapologetically, and brilliantly you.

SUCCESS PRINCIPLE

Being True to You - Authenticity is the foundation of true success. When you align with your core values, passions, and purpose, you create a life that feels fulfilling, meaningful, and uniquely yours. Success is not just about achieving goals, it is also about how you achieve them. It is about walking your path with integrity, making choices that reflect who you truly are, and refusing to conform to expectations that do not serve you.

The most respected and impactful leaders in history did not succeed by imitating others. They stood firm in their beliefs, owned their stories, and led with conviction. If you want to build a lasting legacy, you must first know what you stand for. When you embrace your authenticity, you develop the clarity to confidently make decisions, the resilience to overcome challenges, and the magnetism to attract the right people and opportunities into your life.

Success is not about fitting into the world's definition of achievement. It is about creating success on your own terms and having the courage to live it fully.

SUCCESS MINDSET

Living authentically requires intentional action. It is about knowing who you are and about making daily choices that honor your truth. Authenticity is a practice, a way of being that shapes how you show up in the world, how you interact with others, and how you pursue success. It takes courage to stand firm in your values, especially in a world that often pressures you to conform. But when you commit to authenticity, you build a foundation for lasting fulfillment, meaningful relationships, and purpose-driven success.

To integrate authenticity into your daily life, start by practicing radical self-awareness. Regularly check in with yourself and ask: *Am I living in alignment with my values? Am I making choices that feel true to who I am?* If something feels off, permit yourself to adjust. Living authentically also means setting boundaries and saying no to things that do not serve your highest purpose. Protect your energy, prioritize what matters most, and surround yourself with people who encourage you to be your truest self.

Another key to authenticity is vulnerability. Be willing to share your real thoughts, feelings, and experiences without fear of judgment. The more you show up as your true self, the more you inspire others to do the same. Lastly, take bold action toward your dreams. When you live authentically, you stop waiting for permission and create a life reflecting your deepest aspirations.

Authenticity is not just a mindset. It is a commitment to honoring who you are in every moment. When you fully embrace it, you unlock a level of confidence, clarity, and success that is both powerful and undeniable.

Here are the cornerstones of an authentic and genuine way of being that keeps you true to you:

1. Define Your Core Values

- Success without alignment feels empty. Take time to identify what truly matters to you. *Is it freedom, creativity, service, integrity, connection?* When your decisions align with your values, life becomes more fulfilling.

2. Own Your Story

- Your journey, including its challenges, is what makes you unique. Instead of hiding from it, embrace it. Your experiences are your strength, not your weakness.

3. Set Boundaries

- Being true to yourself means protecting your energy and saying no to things that do not reflect your values. Success is about staying committed to what truly matters to you, instead of people-pleasing.

4. Pursue What Lights You Up

- Passion is a clue to your purpose. If something excites you, follow it. Do not let fear or societal expectations keep you from exploring what truly fulfills you.

5. Let Go of Comparison

- Your journey is uniquely yours. Stop measuring your success by someone else's timeline. Focus on your growth, your fulfillment, and your definition of success.

6. Surround Yourself with Authentic People

- Build relationships with people who celebrate your true self. The company you keep influences your mindset, energy, and success. Choose wisely.

Authenticity is not just about personal fulfillment, it is the foundation for everything you will build. When you love who you are and see the value in your work, you become a beacon for others. Your confidence inspires, your authenticity attracts, and your purpose-driven actions create a massive ripple effect that encourages those around you to embrace their own truth. That allows the right people to find you, the right doors to open, and the right opportunities to align. Success becomes natural because you are simply being you.

SUCCESS CODE: **BE AUTHENTIC**

The greatest success you will ever achieve is becoming the fullest expression of who you truly are.

CHAPTER 21

THE FINAL KEY TO THE MILLENNIAL SUCCESS CODE

Unlocking Purpose, Power,

and Personal Legacy.

A s you step forward from this book and into the next phase of your journey, I challenge you to take everything you have learned and apply it with confidence. Define your values and live by them. Chase your passions without hesitation. Speak your truth with conviction. Surround yourself with those who uplift and challenge you. And most of all, never shrink yourself to fit into places you have outgrown.

Your success is already within you. Your potential is already limitless. Your impact is already in motion. Now, go out there and own it.

In this final section of *The Millennial Success Code*, you have uncovered the most powerful truths about what it means to achieve success, lead with impact, stand for something greater than yourself, and build a legacy that extends beyond personal gain. These codes were never just about individual success. They were about the bigger picture, the world you are helping to shape through your actions, leadership, and commitment to positive change.

The Honorables Values Code reminds us that leadership is rooted in integrity, empathy, and a commitment to uplifting others. True success is not measured solely by personal achievements, but by the positive impact you have on the world around you. Leadership isn't about titles; it's about using your influence to empower others, foster collaboration, and build a lasting legacy. The difference you make in the lives of those you touch is the true marker of your leadership.

The Evolution of Success Code challenges you to view success as a journey, not just a destination. It's about growth, learning, and continuously evolving. The world is always changing, and the key to thriving is embracing transformation. Resilience, adaptability, and innovation are the forces that propel you forward. When you embrace change rather than resist it, you unlock new possibilities and opportunities that you never imagined.

The Unity Code proved that success is not a solo pursuit. The greatest achievements come from collaboration, shared vision, and a commitment to diversity and inclusion. By fostering unity in your workplace, your community, and your relationships, you create an environment where everyone has the chance to rise.

And finally, the **Being True to You Code** revealed the most powerful truth. Success is meaningless if it does not align with who you truly are. Your authenticity is your greatest asset. When you show up as your real, unapologetic self, you become a force to be reckoned with, one that inspires, empowers, and leads with integrity.

You now hold the blueprint for success, in your personal life and in the impact you will create in the world around you. The codes you have read are more than just principles. They are the foundation for a life of purpose, passion, and fulfillment.

CHAPTER 22

OWNING YOUR SUCCESS

Success Is Not A Secret;

It's A Choice.

You have now learned the many *Millennial Success Code*, a framework designed to help you unlock your highest potential, navigate challenges confidently, and create a life that aligns with your values and aspirations. Throughout this book, you have explored codes that empower you to think differently, embrace change, and lead with impact. Now, the final key is you must own your success.

Success is not something that happens to you; it is something you create.

No matter where you started, what setbacks you have faced, and what fears may still linger, you now hold the tools to rewrite your future. This book was never about giving you permission to succeed but rather showing you that the power was *already within you.*

The codes in this book were not just principles. *They were steps toward transformation.*

In part one, you learned that success starts within. Mindset is everything. You discovered the importance of adaptability, resilience, and continuous learning. You learned that your habits, thoughts, and willingness to evolve shape your success trajectory. Success is not about luck or circumstance; it is about *how* you train your mind to see opportunities, push through obstacles, and commit to lifelong growth. The strongest foundation for success is the one you build internally.

In part two, you saw that success is not just about skills but about how you choose to show up in the world. You explored what it means to lead, to be entrepreneurial in your thinking, and to make decisions that align with your core values. You now understand that true success is built on integrity, self-awareness, and the ability to take action with conviction. It is not about following a set path but about carving your own. You learned that leadership is not reserved for titles, entrepreneurship is not just for business owners, and your daily choices determine your impact.

In part three, you expanded your vision beyond yourself. You embraced the power of impact, unity, and authenticity. You saw that your success is not just about what you achieve. It is about how you uplift others, contribute to something greater, and create a legacy that lasts. You learned that success is most meaningful when shared, that true leadership brings people together, and authenticity is the key to creating a life and career that truly fulfills you. When you align your actions with your higher purpose, you do not just succeed. You leave the world better than you found it.

Now, with *The Millennial Success Code* in your hands, you have everything you need to take bold, decisive action toward your future. The journey doesn't end here. *This is only the beginning.*

CREATING A BLUEPRINT FOR SUCCESS THAT IS UNIQUELY YOURS

Knowing the codes is not enough. Now, you must apply them. You cannot wait for the perfect moment, for permission, or for someone else to show you the way. Everything you need is already *within you.* The clarity, the drive, the potential, it is all there and waiting for you to trust it. Success comes from action, making decisions that align with your values and having the courage to take the next step even when you do not have all the answers. You now have the tools, the mindset, and the vision; it is up to you to use them to shape your desired future.

If you distill all of what you have learned to the core of the codes, this is what they exemplify:

Define your success: stop chasing someone else's version of it and start creating a life that aligns with who you truly are.

Take action: the most successful people are not the ones who have all the answers, but they are the ones who take bold steps forward even when they are uncertain.

Own your story: stop hiding from your truth. The lessons you have learned, the challenges you have faced, and the dreams you hold matter. Your story *is* your power.

Lead with impact: success is not just about what you achieve. It is about how you inspire others, uplift those around you, and contribute to the world in a meaningful way.

Success is not for the lucky, the privileged, or the chosen few; it is for those who decide to rise.

THE MILLENNIAL SUCCESS CODE
IS NOW YOURS

The Millennial Success Code is now yours. This book may be ending, but your journey is just beginning. The path to success, fulfillment, and impact is not reserved for a select few, but available to anyone willing to take the first step. You have the knowledge, the tools, and the mindset. Now, it is the time to act.

Heartfelt leadership is not just about achieving goals. It is about transforming yourself to transform the world around you. It is leading purposefully, lifting others as you rise, and refusing to settle for anything less than your best. Every code you have learned is a tool. Every lesson is a key. Every insight is a stepping stone.

Foster good habits, be patient with yourself, and trust that everything is unfolding at the right time. Every challenge, lesson, and victory shapes you into the person you are meant to become. I began this book by addressing the impatience of millennials, the drive to succeed quickly, to achieve more, and to make an impact now. But real success is not a race; it is a journey. The most extraordinary leaders, creators, and innovators did not build their legacies overnight. They nurtured their vision, refined their skills, and allowed their purpose to unfold in their own time.

You have years ahead of you to refine your vision, grow into the leader you are meant to be, and create a lasting impact. Each day is a precious gift, an opportunity to take one more step toward the life you envision. Do not rush your success; savor it. Learn from it. Let it unfold gracefully, knowing that every setback, every pivot, and every breakthrough is working in your favor.

Trust that the path ahead leads you exactly where you need to go. The dreams you hold, the purpose that calls you forward, the impact you are meant to make; these are not accidental. They are your unique blueprint for success. Follow them boldly. Honor them fully. And never forget that you were made for greatness.

The world is waiting for you to step fully into your potential. Go forward with confidence. Take action with purpose. Lead with authenticity.

You are not just capable of success; *you are destined for it.*

Now, step forward and own it.

"Success is not about becoming someone else. It is about becoming the truest, boldest, most unstoppable version of yourself."

CHAPTER 23

YOUR JOURNEY BEGINS RIGHT NOW

Step Into Your Success

A s we conclude this journey through the pages of inspiration, enlightenment, and empowerment, I am reminded of the profound transformations we have witnessed together. From exploring the intricacies of millennial success to delving into the depths of personal growth and societal impact, we have traversed landscapes of inspiration and insight.

But our journey together does not need to end here. It merely can transition into a new phase of empowerment and action. Everything you have read in these pages has prepared you for what comes next. You now understand that success is not just about external achievements but internal alignment. It is about how you think, show up in the world, and use your success to uplift others.

This is where you take the codes and put them into practice. Define your values and live by them. Chase your passions without hesitation.

Speak your truth with conviction. Surround yourself with people who challenge and inspire you. And most of all, never shrink yourself to fit into places you have outgrown.

If there is one thing I want you to take away from this book, it is this, you are capable of more than you have ever imagined, you do not need permission to be great, you do not need to wait for the perfect moment—everything you need is *already* inside of you.

YOU ARE NOT ALONE

For years, I have worked with millennials like you, people with big dreams, untapped potential, and a hunger for more. As a coach and trainer, I have helped individuals break through limitations, build unshakable confidence, and create success on their own terms. I have seen firsthand what happens when someone fully commits to their growth. Their mindset shifts, their opportunities expand, and they step into a level of success they once thought impossible.

I know that transformation does not happen overnight, and it does not happen alone. It requires continuous learning, mentorship, and the right environment to grow. That is why I have created multiple ways to support you beyond this book. Whether you are looking for personal coaching, leadership development, or a community of like-minded achievers, there are many ways you can deepen your success and apply these codes at an even higher level.

Your journey is yours to walk, but you do not have to do it alone. That is why I created *Project One Million*, a movement designed to empower individuals like you to reach their highest potential. Through mentorship, training, and real-world skills, we are helping people break barriers, rewrite their stories, and create lives filled with purpose and success. If you are ready to realize your full potential and take the next step; join the movement, invest in yourself, and step into a future where ambition meets action and the impossible becomes possible.

Within *Project One Million*, our signature program *Be the Best Version of Yourself*™ does more than just teach success principles; it creates opportunities. Not only will you transform your mindset in just three months, you will also gain practical skills in fields like mechanical, electrical, and IT, equipping you for lasting success. More than that, we are creating employment by coaching individuals to become trainers and partners within our company. This is not just about learning to fish; it is about empowering you to provide for your family, uplift your community, and build a future of independence and purpose.

If you are ready to realize your full potential and take the next step I encourage you to join *Project One Million*, become a part of something bigger, and step into a future where ambition meets action and where the impossible becomes possible.

LET'S STAY CONNECTED

Transformation happens through collaboration. It happens when you surround yourself with the right people, mindset, and opportunities. It requires continuous learning, mentorship, and the right environment to grow. That is why I have created multiple ways to support you beyond this book. Whether you are looking for personal coaching, leadership development, or a community of like-minded achievers, there are many ways you can deepen your success and apply these codes at an even higher level.

I also invite you to listen to my podcast, *Inspirational Journeys through Life with STRAIGHTALKWITHNOLAN,* where I dive deep into real conversations about success, resilience, and leadership. Here, you will find stories of individuals who have transformed their lives, strategies for overcoming setbacks, and the motivation you need to keep pushing forward.

If you want to amplify your success to the next level, I welcome you to book a call with me. Let's explore how we can work together to accelerate your growth, build your confidence, and craft a life of purpose. I work with individuals from all walks of life, and my mission is to ensure that each person I mentor steps into the best version of themselves.

Beyond personal success, I believe in creating impact. If you want to be part of something bigger, I invite you to explore our initiatives that uplift communities. Through our excursions, we are empowering the Deaf community, and soon, we will expand our reach to support the blind. In the coming year, we will take on new challenges, push the limits, and continue climbing—both literally and metaphorically—to raise awareness and create change.

No matter where you are in your journey, know that we all need someone to believe in us, to show us the way, and to remind us of our potential. Allow me to be that for you. Let's walk this path together and make your success story one worth telling.

As you close this book, I invite you to reflect on the principles and strategies unveiled within its pages. Let them serve as guiding lights on your path to greatness. Embrace change, cultivate resilience, and dare to dream boldly. Your journey toward personal and professional fulfillment awaits, and I am confident that you will rise to meet it with courage and conviction.

Your next step will be the most important one.

I do not just want this book to be something you read and set aside. I want it to be a catalyst for something bigger in your life.

So, as you close these pages, I leave you with this:

You are powerful.
You are capable.
You are worthy of every dream you hold in your heart.

Now, go out there and make it real.

Your best version is waiting. Go create it!

Thank you for embarking on this transformative journey with me. May your life be filled with boundless possibilities and continue to inspire others with your greatness.

Much Love and Light,
Nolan

LEADERSHIP, IMPACT, AND LEGACY

Own Your Power, Step Into Leadership, And Define
The Legacy You're Building.

You've built your foundation and stepped into aligned action. Now the question is—*what are you building that will outlast you?* Your leadership isn't about titles or being in the spotlight. It's about how you impact others with your presence, your vision, and your choices. This is where purpose becomes power.

Leadership begins with how you lead yourself. Legacy starts with how you love others. This is your moment to recognize that you already have what it takes to make a meaningful difference.

Reflection Prompts:

· What does leadership mean to me right now?

_____

_____

· How do I want to be remembered—not just someday, but tomorrow?

_____

_____

· Who have I already impacted with my growth, even in small ways?

_____

_____

- What cause, idea, or mission moves me to act with courage?

_____

_____

- Where do I need to step up and trust myself more fully?

_____

_____

Action Steps:

- Write a personal leadership statement in one bold sentence.

_____

_____

- Name three people you can uplift, mentor, or support this month.

_____

_____

- Choose one cause or movement that matters to you. Research how to get involved.

_____

_____

- Reflect on your unique strengths. How can they solve a problem in the world?

_____

_____

REFLECTION

Embodying the Success Code

You made it. You've walked through the journey of self-discovery, aligned action, and expanded purpose. You've reflected, stretched, questioned, and grown along the way. But this isn't the end. It's a beginning. What you've read is a blueprint—but what you do with it now will shape your reality.

This section is here for you to look back, capture what moved you, and define what comes next. Take your time. Get honest. Speak from your heart. And know that everything you've learned is already within you—waiting to be lived.

YOUR PERSONAL CODE REVIEW

Which of the Success Codes resonated with you most deeply?

Why did it speak to you?

_____

_____

_____

_____

_____

_____

_____

_____

Which code felt like the easiest to adopt into your life?

How are you already living it?

_____

_____

_____

_____

_____

_____

_____

Which code felt the most challenging?

Why? What resistance came up?

_____

_____

_____

_____

_____

_____

_____

Which code do you want to fully embody in the next 90 days?

What actions will support that?

_____

_____

_____

_____

_____

_____

_____

_____

INTEGRATION PROMPTS

This section is about going deeper. You've absorbed a lot of powerful ideas, but now it's time to reflect on how they've landed in your heart and how they're shaping your path forward. These prompts are designed to help you connect the dots between what you've read and what you're ready to live. Take your time. Be honest. This is where insight becomes transformation.

What beliefs about success have I let go of through reading this book?

_____

_____

_____

_____

_____

What new definitions of success have I created for myself?

_____

_____

_____

_____

_____

_____

How have I grown emotionally, mentally, or spiritually—while moving through these chapters?

_____

_____

_____

_____

_____

What surprised me about myself as I reflected on these ideas?

_____

_____

_____

_____

_____

What is one small shift I can make today to start living the life I truly want?

_____

_____

_____

_____

YOUR COMMITMENT TO ACTION

Insight is powerful, but real change happens when you take aligned action. This section invites you to turn inspiration into movement. Small steps taken with intention create lasting momentum. What you commit to here doesn't have to be perfect—it just has to be true to you. Let this be your moment to declare what's next with clarity, courage, and conviction.

Success doesn't come from reading, it comes from doing. Choose three inspired actions to take from here:

1. _____

2. _____

3. _____

Who do I want to share this journey with?

(Mentor, peer, coach, friend—growth is amplified when shared.)

_____

_____

_____

_____

_____

_____

_____

What will I do to celebrate my growth so far?

(Acknowledge how far you've come.)

_____

_____

_____

_____

_____

_____

_____

_____

_____

_____

_____

_____

_____

_____

_____

_____

_____

_____

LEGACY VISIONING

You are a leader, even if you don't wear that title yet. You're someone whose presence, courage, and compassion can shift the energy in any space. Let's connect to your vision for lasting impact.

What do I want my legacy to be?

_____

_____

_____

_____

_____

_____

What values do I want people to remember me by?

_____

_____

_____

_____

_____

What one message do I hope to pass on to the next generation?

_____

_____

_____

_____

_____

_____

_____

What can I do today that aligns with the legacy I want to build tomorrow?

_____

_____

_____

_____

_____

_____

_____

_____

A FINAL WORD FROM NOLAN

Success isn't a finish line. It's a rhythm, a state of alignment, a way of showing up for your life. The codes you've explored in this book are yours now. Let them guide you, stretch you, and ground you. Keep showing up. Keep learning. Keep leading from within.

You have everything it takes. *You always have.*

WORK WITH NOLAN PILLAY

If this book has resonated with you, imagine what we could achieve together. Whether you are looking for personal coaching, leadership development, mindset mastery, or even opportunities to join our mission, we can connect and create an impact in many ways. Whether you want to dive deeper into mindset mastery, leadership development, or personal coaching, there is a place for you and me to work together.

Join the Movement: *Project One Million*

At *Project One Million*, we transform lives by reshaping mindsets and equipping individuals with real-world skills. This is more than just a program; it is a movement to empower, uplift, and create sustainable change. You can be part of this journey by working with me directly, becoming a trainer, or even launching your own initiative within our ecosystem.

Coaching Program: *Be the Best Version of Yourself™*

If you are ready to break through limitations, master your mindset, and step into a life of purpose and success, my coaching programs are designed for you. Through one-on-one coaching, group sessions, and transformational courses; I will help you rewire your thoughts, conquer self-doubt, and achieve your biggest goals.

Tune into the Podcast: *Inspirational Journeys Through Life with StraightTalkWithNolan*

Transformation happens through conversation, through real talk, and through hearing the stories of those who have walked the path before you. That is exactly why I created my podcast, *STRAIGHTTALKWITHNOLAN.*

In each episode, I dive deep into success, resilience, leadership, and impact. You will hear powerful stories, practical strategies, and the motivation you need to keep pushing forward. If this book resonated with you, I guarantee you will find even more inspiration tuning into the podcast.

Work Directly with Me

If you want to take your personal growth to the next level, I offer private coaching and mentorship for those ready to accelerate their success. Together, we will:

✓ Rewire limiting beliefs.

✓ Build unstoppable confidence.

✓ Set powerful goals and create a clear roadmap for success.

✓ Elevate your mindset to match the level of success you are meant for.

I also offer corporate training, leadership development, and keynote speaking for organizations looking to empower their teams with the winning mindset, resilience, and motivation needed to thrive.

Make an Impact Together

Beyond personal success, I believe in creating lasting change. If you are someone who wants to be part of a movement that lifts up others, I invite you to explore our global initiatives.

We are pushing limits, breaking barriers, and proving that impact knows no boundaries.

If you want to be part of this journey, whether by getting involved, supporting our missions, or joining us for one of our legendary excursions, I would love to have you alongside me.

Reach out and Collaborate

There are many ways we can grow together. Whether you want one-on-one coaching, group mentorship, corporate leadership training, or to join *Project One Million*, the next step is yours to take.

Email:

nolan@straighttalkwithnolan.com

Websites:

https://nolanpillay360.com/

https://straighttalkwithnolan.com/

https://bethebestversionofyourself.co.za/

https://project1million.co.za/

Social Media:

Facebook: nolan.pillay.37

Instagram: iamnolanpillay

LinkedIn: nolanpillay

Human Mindset Specialist | Global Award Winner | Founder of StraightTalkWithNolan & Be the BEST Version of YOURSELF Foundation

AUTHOR BIOGRAPHY

Nolan Pillay is a Global Award Winner (Las Vegas May 2024), Influential Men Awardee, Human Mindset Specialist and Life Coach, Professional Speaker and Consultant, Enlightened Warrior, 2x International Best-Selling Author, and Philanthropist. He is also the dynamic founder of *StraightTalkWithNolan* (Pty) Ltd and the Non-Profit organization *Be the BEST version of YOURSELF Foundation*. His latest online course, *Obstacles Make You Stronger*, addresses critical topics such as mental wellness, depression, suicide, limiting beliefs, and how we, as humans, have the strength to rise above life's challenges with confidence and ease.

Nolan's core focus is on African youth. He has set an ambitious Moonshot: "Transform 1 million lives in Africa, starting with our teens and young adults by enhancing their mindsets and thought processes through our Coaching, Authentic Leadership, and Personal Mastery programs."

Having grown up in humble circumstances, Nolan experienced poverty and hunger firsthand. He did homework by candlelight, worked multiple jobs to provide for his family, and supported himself through school. After over two decades as an SAP IT consultant, he transitioned to his true calling—empowering others through mindset transformation.

As a philanthropist, Nolan and the *Be the BEST version of YOURSELF* foundation work on several impactful projects. In 2022, they climbed Mt. Kilimanjaro to raise funds for children born Deaf, with five of the seven climbers being from the Deaf community—an initiative to bridge the gap between the hearing and Deaf communities. The team raised funds and gifted five children with hearing aids, allowing them to live a normal life. This year, they again climbed Mt. Kilimanjaro, focusing on Cancer and Mental Wellness awareness, along with their upcoming *Skills Village*.

Nolan is also remembered for his 2019 Mt. Kilimanjaro climb, where he raised funds to provide girls in rural areas with access to sanitary pads, a cause he passionately believes should be universally supported.

In January 2021, Nolan had a near-death experience battling COVID-19 pneumonia. This harrowing ordeal became a turning point. Through his daily practices, mindset techniques, and unwavering will to live, he not only survived but emerged stronger. This experience inspired him to write his first book, *My COVID Journey - Techniques and Mind Hacks that got me through it*, sharing his journey and offering readers mind hacks and resilience techniques. More than just a personal story, the book empowers others to confront life's obstacles head-on, providing tools to overcome health challenges and adversity. His powerful message helps families who have lost loved ones to COVID-19 find peace while also equipping individuals with actionable strategies to build mental strength.

Nolan firmly believes that contributing and collaborating with others is a fulfilling service that uplifts communities and the world at large. He invites you to join him on this journey of empowerment and transformation.

Nolan's mantra, *It's Time to Live and Serve Our Purpose*, is not just a phrase, but a guiding principle that echoes through his life and work. He hopes it will inspire you to discover and live your own purpose.

ACKNOWLEDGEMENTS

I would like to express my deepest gratitude to Lady JB Owen and the entire Ignite Publishing™ team for walking this transformative journey with me. Lady JB, your passion for storytelling and your unwavering belief in the power of words to ignite change have been a constant source of inspiration throughout this process. Your visionary leadership and support have brought this book to life, and your belief in me and what I stand for has fueled my drive to make a meaningful impact. You saw not just the words on the page but the purpose behind them, and for that, I am truly honored to have shared this journey with you.

As we worked through each chapter, there were times when the process felt overwhelming. The task of reflecting, revising, and perfecting my message seemed daunting, but your wisdom helped me see things differently. You reminded me that this process was not just about writing a book but also about deepening my understanding of my work, mission, and voice. Those words allowed everything to shift for me. What once felt like an uphill climb began to make sense, and it empowered me to become a great student of my own journey. This deeper connection to my work would not have been possible without your guidance and insight, and for that, I am truly grateful.

To my lead editor, Mimi Safiyah, your incredible talent, dedication, and attention to detail have been invaluable. From the very first draft to the final manuscript, your thoughtful guidance and insightful feedback have shaped my words into something greater than I could have ever imagined on my own. Your patience, understanding, and commitment to my book have made this process smoother and more rewarding than I could have hoped for.

Together with the entire Ignite Publishing team, you have turned what once was a vision into a reality. This book stands as a testament to your hard work, creativity, and the belief that every story has the power to inspire and transform. For that, I am eternally thankful. Thank You.

I would also like to acknowledge my wife, Seema, and my children, Alicia and Tre, for their constant support and motivation. Your love and belief in me have been my anchor through every challenge and triumph. Seema, your unwavering encouragement, patience, and understanding have carried me through even the toughest moments of this journey. Your strength has allowed me to stay focused and push forward, and your belief in my work has fueled my own confidence and determination.

Alicia and Tre, you have been a constant source of joy and motivation. Your smiles, faith in me, and endless support have kept me grounded and reminded me of what truly matters. Knowing that you are proud of me means more than words can express, and it has driven me to be the best version of myself, not only as a writer but as a father.

This journey would not have been possible without each of you by my side. You have been my greatest source of strength, and for that, I am endlessly thankful.

Much Love and Light,
Nolan

REFERENCE

Websites:

https://nolanpillay360.com/

https://straighttalkwithnolan.com/

https://bethebestversionofyourself.co.za/

https://project1million.co.za/

Social Websites:

Facebook: https://www.facebook.com/nolan.pillay.37

Instagram: https://www.instagram.com/iamnolanpillay/

LinkedIn: https://www.linkedin.com/in/nolanpillay/

Programs done by me:

Thriving Minds, Thriving Results

https://www.udemy.com/course/thriving-minds-thriving-results/?referralCode=E5BDE47A9230678A8C86

Obstacles Make You Stronger

https://www.udemy.com/course/obstacles_make_me_stronger/?referralCode=6E435395FCA7ED07237D

Books written:

My COVID Journey - Techniques and Mindhacks that got me through it.

https://www.amazon.com/My-Covid-Journey-Techniques-through-ebook/dp/B09GPXTXSK

Podcasts:

Inspirational Journeys through Life with StraightTalkwithNolan

https://www.youtube.com/@nolanpillay360

Books to read:

Think and Grow Rich - Napoleon Hill

Long walk to Freedom - Nelson Mandela

The Power of Now - Eckhart Tolle

Autobiography of a Yogi - Paramahansa Yogananda

REFERENCES

[1] American Psychological Association. (2018). Stress in America: Generation Z

[2] Journal of the American Medical Association, 2020

[3] CDC Morbidity and Mortality Weekly Report, 2017

[4] National Sleep Foundation Sleep Health Index, 2019

[5] Physical Activity Council Annual Participation Report, 2020

TRADEMARKS

Millionaire Mind Intensive™ is a trademark of Success Resources.

Enlightened Warrior Power™ is a trademark of Success Resources.

Train the Trainer with T. Harv Eker™ is a trademark of Success Resources.

Thinking into Results™ is a trademark of Proctor Gallagher Institute.

Paradigm Shift with Bob Proctor™ is a trademark of Proctor Gallagher Institute.

MY Comeback Challenge™ is a trademark of Tony Robbins.

Date with Destiny with Tony Robbins™ is a trademark of Tony Robbins.

Be Extraordinary™ is a trademark of Mindvalley.

Silva UltraMind System™ is a trademark of Mindvalley.

Super Brain™ is a trademark of Mindvalley.

Speak & Inspire™ is a trademark of Mindvalley.

Life Visioning Mastery™ is a trademark of Mindvalley.

Mastering Authentic Networking™ is a trademark of Mindvalley.

Personal Mastery™ is a trademark of Mindvalley.

Think and Grow Rich™ is a trademark of The Napoleon Hill Foundation.

Ignite Your Solo Book™ is a trademark of Ignite Publishing.

Be the Best Version of Yourself™ it's a trademark of straighttalkwithnolan

Ignite Publishing™ is a trademark of Ignite Publishing.

Mindvalley™ is a trademark of Mindvalley.

Girls Who Code™ is a trademark of Girls Who Code, Inc.

Apple™ is a trademark of Apple Inc.

Microsoft™ is a trademark of Microsoft Corporation.

Google™ is a trademark of Google LLC.

Slack™ is a trademark of Slack Technologies, LLC.

LinkedIn™ is a trademark of LinkedIn Corporation.

Atlassian™ is a trademark of Atlassian Corporation Plc.

Buffer™ is a trademark of Buffer, Inc.

Airbnb™ is a trademark of Airbnb, Inc.

Bumble™ is a trademark of Bumble Inc.

Xbox™ is a trademark of Microsoft Corporation.

Ignite Humanity™ is a trademark of Ignite Publishing.